We should look for someone to eat and drink with before looking for something to eat and drink.

Epicurus (341-270 BC)

www.loveonthemenucookbook.com

www.loveonthemenucookbook.com

Concept and Publishing   Linda Arsenault

Food and Wine Pairings   Alain Dumulong

Art Direction and Graphic Design   Sonia Landry

Chefs   Marie-Hélène Reid
Sara Coupry

Photography   Rodolf Noël

French to English Translation   Pina Broccoli Anaia

Print Management   Dominique Lemire and Brigitte Lestage
IntraMedia, division of Datamark Systems

From the same publisher:
Farmers in Chef Hats of Île d'Orléans
(www.farmersinchefhats.com)

L.A. Communication inc.
All rights reserved
Legal deposit – Bibliothèque et Archives nationales du Québec, 2010
Legal deposit – National Library of Canada, 2010
ISBN 978-2-9809721-2-6

Miss chocolate praline

Miss chocolate praline
Flashes almond eyes, hazelnuts
Her body is the colour of chocolate spread
While the naughty watch and lick their lips
They drift into a world of gluttony

Miss chocolate praline
Entices the taste buds like a cocoa bean
Her heart has a melting brown middle
To be nibbled, to be savoured, to be damned
With the last piece, the ultimate torment
A dazzling display under her tin foil dress

Miss chocolate praline
Lets teeth sink into her body
Her gingerbread neighbours are jealous
And caramel is a little too gooey
Her striking flavours, leaving you tongue-tied
Her warm liquid, sticky sweet on the palate.

Nathalie BRULE
www.octopussy.rmc.fr
(Translated from the French)

Following my first recipe book – *Farmers in Chef Hats** – which was published with the participation of my farmer friends from my beloved island of Île d'Orléans and chef Philip Rae, I now present this more urban book. It is still all about food of course, but this time the focus is on sensual cooking.

Just what is sensual cooking? Or should I say sensory? It is cooking full of feelings and emotions, nourished by a scented bubble bath, a relaxing massage, sexy music, a titillating cocktail and an inviting meal, accompanied by good wine and a lover, most definitely!

And what about the products with aphrodisiac properties? Well, nothing serious! Just rumours and a glimmer of hope! But they are fun, suggestive, tasty and good for your health... and we used them as much as possible. Some products have been considered aphrodisiacs for hundreds of years due to their composition. Others have acquired this status through their shape and texture.

Sensual cooking is made for two. Touch, hearing, smell, taste and sight... all five senses are evoked before, during and after the meal. There is no cooking without senses and no sensation without passion!

Love on the Menu is much more than a recipe book. Explore all the chapters: Hit Parade, Preludes, Love Potions, Bits and Bites, Starters, Essentials and Guilty Pleasures. You will find a host of ingredients to whet your appetite and spice up that romantic meal.

Linda Arsenault
www.loveonthemenucookbook.com

* www.farmersinchefhats.com: Winner of the Best Local Cookery Book in the World in 2007.

The Team

It's not often one has total freedom to choose their team members. It was a rare privilege to work with such competent people, specifically chosen for their kindness, sense of humour, dedication, generosity and friendship. This is the gift I gave myself and wish to share with you now.

The epicurean: Alain Dumulong, a loving and sensual man, quite simply passionate in all senses and by all senses. When I met him almost ten years ago at a business lunch, he spoke to me about geography, agriculture, weather, history… in fact, he was talking about wine. His passion, knowledge and work ethic are the reasons I asked him to team up with me to create this book. He is responsible for the food and wine pairings and the Love Potions chapter. He was an extraordinary collaborator in all aspects.

The art director: Sonia Landry is responsible for the look and design of this book. She took part in the *Farmers in Chef Hats* adventure and is closely linked to the Best Local Cookery Book in the World award in 2007. With Sonia, "there always has to be something going on and intensity and drive are a must or it isn't worth doing". A creative, reserved, sensual and talented woman, as well as a terrific collaborator, she wasted no time in accepting my invitation to work on this daring project. She invested all her time and talent in putting her own stamp on it.

The chefs: Marie-Hélène Reid and Sara Coupry, two young women who decided to leave the great restaurant kitchens and open their own. Friends for 20 years, they have been at the helm of Haricot Traiteur since 2008. They humbly agreed to take part in this adventure full of uncertainties. Concocting recipes, participating in the culinary concept and design… they successfully rose to the challenge. Their future looks promising.

The photographer: Rodolf Noël is both funny and serious. He is extremely talented and methodical, but also laid back and relaxed. He's a real gem! In addition to taking all the photos in the book, he participated in the concept of the sensual and culinary photos and added his own touch to the project. It goes without say that his 30 years of experience with lights and cameras have earned him an enviable reputation.

The translator: Pina Broccoli Anaia was part of the first adventure, the *Farmers in Chef Hats* book. Born to a family of restaurateurs and passionate about cooking, she is completely devoted to her work and has the necessary skills to transform a French text into the language of Shakespeare. She knows just how to find the right word to retain the essence of what is being conveyed. And with a name like Broccoli… she was meant to write about food!

We are thrilled to have participated in *Love on the Menu*. Both of us being young chefs, this bold challenge put our knowledge, creativity and innovative spirit to the test. Cooking plays a very important role in our lives. Our simple cooking style, using quality local products, aims to tantalize the palate through the sheer pleasure of tasting and eating well. For us, sensual cooking is found in the aromas, colours and textures of various foods, sometimes even in their shape. Cooking as a couple is an art, a form of expression and togetherness, an opportunity to transform the kitchen into a saucy playing field where they learn to create an inextricable link with the senses.

Happy cooking, bon appétit and above all... have fun!

Marie-Hélène Reid and Sara Coupry
Haricot Traiteur
www.haricottraiteur.com

Food and Wine Pairings

Like love, a successful food and wine pairing must bring forth pleasure and strong sensations. It is based on the high quality relationship between aromas, flavours and textures in a compatible framework, an intimate blend, an osmosis so to speak.

To assist you in your quest for pleasure... in food, there are several factors worthy of consideration. The basic ingredients, sauce, cooking method, spices, among others, play a vital role in optimizing the quality of food and wine pairings. A successful pairing must suit your tastes and personal preferences. However, if you dare step out of your comfort zone, you will be surprised at what you find. Basically, there is no golden rule for choosing a wine to accompany your meal. After all, isn't the very best wine the one that's your all-time favourite?

Pairings

Each recipe is followed by three types of wine recommendations. The first is a **"Classic"** pairing with the aromas and dominant flavours of the meal. The **"Love at First Taste"** recommendation is based on personal tasting experiences. Lastly, there is the **"Libertine"** tasting journey... almost illicit but every bit as pleasurable as the first two. Novice, budding connoisseur or expert wine taster... there's something in it for everyone, including selecting a wine to suit all budgets and cravings. If necessary, you can ask your local wine merchant to recommend any new arrivals that meet the criteria of the food and wine pairings in this book.

Love Potions

I have also recommended 12 cocktails that were specially created from suggestive or aphrodisiac ingredients. The cocktails are conducive to relaxation but can also make meal preparation more exciting. They are easy to prepare. Anyone can do it. Have fun trying them. They're absolutely delicious!

Happy tasting!

Alain Dumulong

My passion is wine. It's always been on the table. But it now occupies a prime spot on my bedside table.

Hit Parade

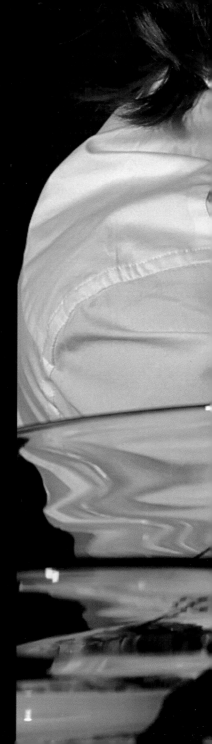

Song	Artist
Like You'll Never See Me Again	Alicia Keys
To Know Him Is To Love Him	Amy Winehouse
All I Ask of You	Barbra Streisand
Wicked Way	Benjamin Taylor
Meet Me Halfway	Black Eyed Peas
Slave To Love	Bryan Ferry
You Belong To Me	Carla Bruni
I Believe In You	Cat Power
Wicked Game	Chris Isaak
Bubbly	Colbie Caillat
Take a Look At Yourself	Coverdale Page
Soldier of Fortune	Deep Purple
Useless	Depeche Mode
Peel Me a Grape	Diana Krall
I Feel Love	Donna Summer
Save a Prayer	Duran Duran
Are You Lonesome Tonight	Elvis Presley
Principles of Lust	Enigma
Wonderful Tonight	Eric Clapton
Something Stupid	Frank Sinatra
Turn Your Love Around	George Benson
I Want Your Sex	George Michael
I Just Wanna Stop	Gino Vannelli
Shake You Down	Gregory Abbott
I'll Dream of You Again	Harry Connick, Jr
You Sexy Thing	Hot Chocolate
Brown Skin	India.Arie
Need You Tonight	INXS
Somewhere Over the Rainbow	Israel Kamakawiwo'ole
Better Together	Jack Johnson
Would You Mind	Janet Jackson
I'm Yours	Jason Mraz
A Long Walk	Jill Scott
Little Wing	Jimi Hendrix
You Can Leave Your Hat On	Joe Cocker
Sunshine's Better	John Martyn
Cinema Paradiso	Josh Groban & Joshua Bell
I Loves You Porgy	Joshua Bell
Lovin', Touchin', Squeezin'	Journey
Sexuality	k.d. lang
I Kissed a Girl	Katy Perry
Sex on Fire	Kings of Leon
My Funny Valentine	Kristin Chenoweth
Sofa Rockers	Kruder & Dorfmeister
Slow	Kylie Minogue
Stairway to Heaven	Led Zeppelin
I Belong To You	Lenny Kravitz
Erotica (Sex Remix)	Madonna
Sexual Healing	Marvin Gaye
Angel	Massive Attack

Song	Artist
I Just Can't Stop Loving You	Michael Jackson
Lovin' You	Minnie Riperton
Down On My Knees	Montell Jordan
Slow Down	Morcheeba
Turn Me On	Norah Jones
Too Drunk To Fuck	Nouvelle Vague
The Great Gig in the Sky	Pink Floyd
Sour Times	Portishead
Creep	Radiohead
In the Kitchen	Robert Kelly
Sex Therapy	Robin Thicke
Tonight's the Night	Rod Stewart
No Ordinary Love	Sade
Love Song	Sara Bareilles
I Love You	Sarah McLachlan
Truly, Madly, Deeply	Savage Garden
The First Cut Is the Deepest	Sheryl Crow
You Make Me Feel Brand New	Simply Red
Nothing Compares 2 U	Sinéad O'Connor
6 Underground	Sneaker Pimps
Come Again	Sting & Joshua Bell
Something	The Beatles
It's Your Love	Tim McGraw with Faith Hill
Diggin' on You	TLC
Sex Bomb	Tom Jones
Lovesong	Tori Amos
Slow An' Easy	Whitesnake

Instrumental

Ma Jojo	Alain Lefebvre
Memory	Andrew Lloyd Webber
Leonora's Love Theme	Astor Piazzolla
Golden Lotus	Buddha Bar III (album)
Secret Love	Buddha Bar III (album)
Rêverie	Claude Debussy
Tema d'amore per Nata	Ennio Morricone
Bilitis	Francis Lai
Love Walked In	George Gershwin
Donna non vidi mai	Kaludi Kaludov
Be My Love	Keith Jarrett
Caruso	Lucio Dalla
I Will Wait for You	Michel Legrand
Always and Forever	Pat Metheny
Milonga del Angel	Richard Galliano
Samba Pa Ti	Santana
Fool on the Hill	The Most Romantic Piano

Table of Contents

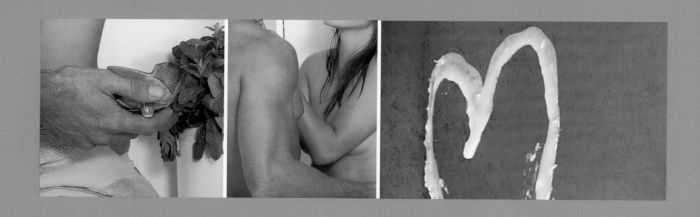

Preludes

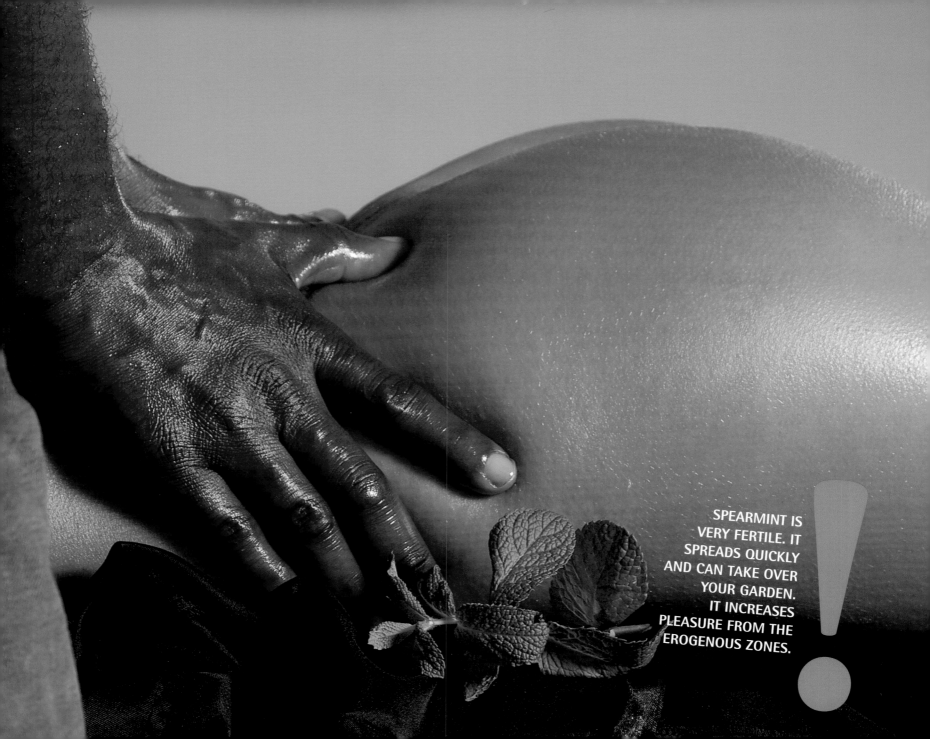

SPEARMINT IS
VERY FERTILE. IT
SPREADS QUICKLY
AND CAN TAKE OVER
YOUR GARDEN.
IT INCREASES
PLEASURE FROM THE
EROGENOUS ZONES.

Massage Oil

Spearmint

Mix:
3/8 cup (95 mL) baby oil
50 drops spearmint essential oil

Almond and Mandarin

Mix:
3/8 cup (95 mL) almond oil
50 drops mandarin essential oil

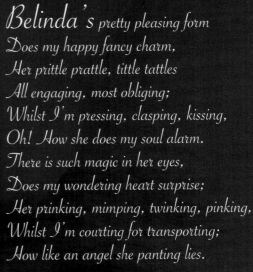

Pure carnal pleasure! A body care concoction for two in a warm, muted ambiance with music chosen to complement the mood. It's the perfect opportunity to savour our Libido Booster cocktail. Like a massage warms the skin, this cocktail will ignite your inner flame.

Belinda's pretty pleasing form
Does my happy fancy charm,
Her prittle prattle, tittle tattles
All engaging, most obliging;
Whilst I'm pressing, clasping, kissing,
Oh! How she does my soul alarm.
There is such magic in her eyes,
Does my wondering heart surprise;
Her prinking, mimping, twinking, pinking,
Whilst I'm courting for transporting;
How like an angel she panting lies.

Anon (set by John Eccles 1668-1735)

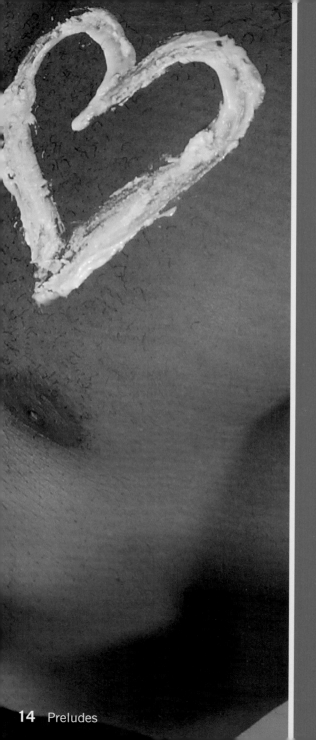

Chocolate Body Paint

Ingredients
1/3 cup (85 mL) honey
1 pinch salt
3 tbsp (45 mL) water
2 tbsp (30 mL) butter
1/4 cup (65 mL) cocoa powder
1-1/2 tsp (7.5 mL) almond essence
1-1/2 tsp (7.5 mL) Grand Marnier®
A paintbrush

Method

Heat honey, salt and water in a small saucepan on medium heat. Set aside.
Whisk in butter, then cocoa powder, almond essence and Grand Marnier,
whisking all the while.
Leave mixture to cool. Keep warm on a chafing dish while using.

The paint can be prepared the day before and reheated in the microwave
for 30 seconds. Then let your creative juices flow!

White Chocolate Paint

Just melt 2 cups (500 mL) of white chocolate chips on low heat,
and let the games begin!

A sweet fortified red wine from the
Roussillon region of France, such as
a Banyuls aged for at least 5 years

Why not complement your prelude with a sweet
fortified red wine to spice up your chocolaty
adventure? This nectar is a strong match with
chocolate...a decadence to be shared!

Another sweet fortified red wine
from Roussillon – a Rivesaltes

A sparkling wine from South West France,
such as a Gaillac, or a Recioto della
Valpolicella from Veneto, Italy

Minty Ylang-Ylang Shaving Cream

Ingredients

2 tbsp (30 mL) honey
1/2 cup (125 mL) boiling water
1/2 cup (125 mL) hard soap, grated
2 tbsp (30 mL) walnut oil
2 tbsp (30 mL) almond oil
8 drops spearmint essential oil
8 drops ylang-ylang essential oil

Method

Dissolve honey in boiling water.
Add grated soap and mix until dissolved.
Add the other ingredients and beat by hand until light and foamy.
Pour the mixture into a cup and leave to harden.
Apply with a shaving brush.

YLANG-YLANG IS A REVITALIZING AND STIMULATING BODY TONIC. IT IS TRULY AN ESSENTIAL OIL.

Avocado and Cucumber Mask

Ingredients

3-inch (7.5 cm) English cucumber, peeled
1/2 avocado, very ripe
3 tbsp (45 mL) honey
2 tbsp (30 mL) 35% cream or whipping cream
2 tbsp (30 mL) glycerine
1 tsp (5 mL) lemon juice
1/4 cup (65 mL) flour

Method

Puree the cucumber and avocado in a small food processor.
Add honey, cream, glycerine and lemon juice.
Mix well to create a creamy texture.
Add flour, one tablespoon at a time, and mix well.
Refrigerate until ready to use.

This recipe can be prepared 48 hours in advance. Apply mixture to the face, relax for 5-10 minutes, then rinse.

AVOCADOS WERE USED TO PROTECT THE SKIN AGAINST DESERT WINDS.

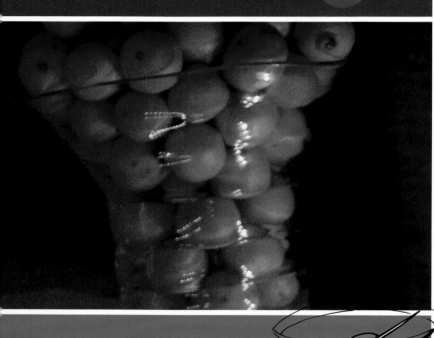

The perfect moment for relaxing before your meal. While soaking in the tub and taking in the enchanting fragrance, why not ask your lover to prepare one of our sweet cocktails, such as the Tongue Tango, and slowly sip it together?

Bubble Bath

Honey and Mandarin

Mix:
3/8 cup (95 mL) baby shampoo, unscented
2 tbsp (30 mL) honey
20 drops mandarin essential oil

Maple and Lavender

Mix:
3/8 cup (95 mL) baby shampoo, unscented
2 tbsp (30 mL) maple syrup
20 drops lavender essential oil

Enticing *fragrant bubbles*
Lather up my latent desire
Gentle and warm calming potion
Softens my skin for my lover

Alain Dumulong
(Translated from the French)

Wine comes in at the mouth
And love comes in at the eye;
That's all we shall know for truth
Before we grow old and die.
I lift the glass to my mouth,
I look at you, and I sigh.

William Butler Yeats (1865-1939)

Love
Potions

Love Potions

These potions were created to tantalize the taste buds, warm the body, awaken the senses and inspire love.

Set the mood! Play some sexy music and let the cocktails enchant you with their sweetness or bewitching powers. The first step on the path to lust...

Definitely to be sipped in tandem!

Peacock Tail

Ingredients per glass

0.5 oz (15 mL) vodka
1 oz (30 mL) Fragoli® wild strawberry liqueur
1 oz (30 mL) lychee juice
Champagne or sparkling wine
1 fresh strawberry, on a swizzle stick

Method

Pour all ingredients, except the champagne
and strawberry, into a shaker half filled with ice.
Shake well.
Pour into a champagne flute and top with
champagne or sparkling wine.
Garnish with the strawberry.

With a kiss, let us set out for an unknown world.
Alfred de Musset (1810-1857)

The only way to get rid of temptation is to yield to it.
Oscar Wilde (1854-1900)

Tongue Tango

Ingredients per glass
1 oz (30 mL) dark rum
1.5 oz (45 mL) Alizé Sunset Passion® fruit liqueur
0.5 oz (15 mL) lime syrup
1.5 oz (45 mL) mango nectar
Raw brown sugar, in crystals
1 slice of lime

Method
Pour all ingredients, except the sugar and slice of lime, into a shaker half filled with ice. Shake well.
Frost the rim of a stemmed glass with brown sugar and add ice cubes.
Pour the mixture into the glass. Garnish with the slice of lime.

On her soft breasts my hand I laid,
And a quick, light impression made;
They with a kindly warmth did glow,
And swelled and seemed to overflow.

Anon (18th century)

Sweet Melons

Ingredients for two glasses
1 ripe cantaloupe, cut in half and seeds removed
1 ripe honeydew melon, cut in half and seeds removed
2 oz (60 mL) Muscat Blanc dessert wine*
1 oz (30 mL) Midori® melon liqueur
Freshly ground pink pepper, 2-3 turns of the pepper mill

Method
Using a melon baller, scoop 5 balls of cantaloupe and
5 balls of honeydew.
Pour dessert wine and melon liqueur into a resealable
plastic bag and add pink pepper. Add cantaloupe and
honeydew balls, seal bag tightly, and leave to macerate
in the fridge for about an hour.
When ready to serve, slide melon balls onto a wooden
skewer or place them in a ramekin.
Serve with a glass of dessert wine chilled at
46°F (8°C).

*   Muscat Blanc dessert wine can be substituted
    with ice wine or ice cider.

Full Moon

Ingredients per glass

1 oz (30 mL) gin
1 oz (30 mL) orange liqueur (Cointreau®,
Triple sec® or Grand Marnier®), to taste
1 oz (30 mL) fresh lemon juice
Ginger ale, to taste
1 lemon rind, on a swizzle stick
1 ground cherry

Method

Pour gin, orange liqueur of preference and lemon juice
into a shaker half filled with ice. Shake well.
Pour into a highball glass half filled with ice.
Top with ginger ale and garnish with a twisted lemon rind
and a ground cherry.

Glowy like the sunlight

Moony like the night

Your bum, I want to bite

Thong Princess

Ingredients per glass
1 oz (30 mL) gin
1 oz (30 mL) Martini® dry white vermouth
1 oz (30 mL) Alizé Gold Passion® fruit liqueur
2 oz (60 mL) cane syrup
4 oz (120 mL) tonic water
1 slice of star fruit

Method
Pour all ingredients, except the tonic water and star fruit, into a shaker half filled with ice. Shake well.
Fill a highball glass with a few ice cubes. Pour the mixture into the glass and add tonic water. Garnish with the slice of star fruit.

Libido Booster

Ingredients per glass
1 oz (30 mL) vodka
1.5 oz (45 mL) crème de menthe blanche (white mint liqueur)
2 oz (60 mL) pear nectar
3 maraschino cherries, on a swizzle stick

Method
Pour all ingredients, except the maraschino cherries, into a shaker half filled with ice. Shake well.
Pour the mixture over two ice cubes in an old fashioned whisky tumbler. Serve with the maraschino cherries.

Breathless

Ingredients per glass
1 oz (30 mL) cinnamon whisky
1.5 oz (45 mL) Griottines® morello cherry liqueur
Carbonated water
3 maraschino cherries, on a swizzle stick

Method
Pour whisky and morello cherry liqueur into a shaker
half filled with ice. Shake well.
Pour the mixture over some ice cubes in a tumbler.
Top with carbonated water to taste.
Garnish with the maraschino cherries.

Ah, give your sweet temptations o'er,
I'll touch those dang'rous lips no more.
What, must we yet fool on?
Ah, now I yield, ah, now I fall,
Ah now I have no breath at all.
And now I'm quite undone.

John Crowne (1641-1712)

Sweet
Temptation

Ingredients per glass
1 oz (30 mL) cognac
1 oz (30 mL) Amaretto di Saronno®
1 oz (30 mL) crème de banane (banana liqueur)
1 oz (30 mL) table cream or single cream
2 drops vanilla extract

Method
Pour all ingredients into a shaker half
filled with ice. Shake well.
Serve in a cognac balloon glass.

Deviance

Ingredients for two glasses
1 oz (30 mL) Amaretto di Saronno®
1 oz (30 mL) Amarula®
Whipped cream

Method

First pour Amaretto di Saronno and then Amarula in a shooter glass. Top with whipped cream.
Bottoms up! Try it with no hands!

Sex Appeal

Ingredients per glass
1 oz (30 mL) Baileys Irish Cream®
0.5 oz (15 mL) sambuca
0.5 oz (15 mL) vodka

Method

Pour all ingredients into a shaker half filled with ice. Shake well.
Serve in a martini glass.

All Fire
and Flame

Ingredients per glass
1 oz (30 mL) grappa
1.5 oz (45 mL) Alizé Red Passion® fruit liqueur
0.5 oz (15 mL) crème de cassis
(black currant liqueur)
1.5 oz (45 mL) freshly squeezed orange juice
1 orange slice

Method
Pour all ingredients, except the orange slice,
into a shaker half filled with ice. Shake well.
Serve on the rocks in an old fashioned whisky glass.
Garnish with the orange slice.

G-Spot

Ingredients per glass
1 oz (30 mL) tequila
0.5 oz (15 mL) Grand Marnier®
1 lime wedge
Fleur de sel (French sea salt), to taste

Method
Pour tequila and Grand Marnier in
a shooter glass.
Choose a spot on your partner's body
to sprinkle some salt. Lick slowly.
Drink a shot and bite into the lime wedge
to suck on the juice.

Bits
and
Bites

And her lips opened amorously, and said--
I wist not what, saving one word – *Delight,*
And all her face was honey to my mouth,
And all her body pasture to mine eyes;
The long lithe arms and hotter hands than fire,
The quivering flanks, hair smelling of the south,
The bright light feet, the splendid supple thighs
And glittering eyelids of my soul's desire.

Algernon Charles Swinburne (1837-1909)

Triangles of Happiness

Filling Ingredients
3 oz (90 g) baby spinach
1 tsp (5 mL) butter
1/4 cup (65 mL) white onion, finely diced
2 tbsp (30 mL) pine nuts
1/2 cup (125 mL) ricotta
8 dried apricots, chopped
Salt and pepper, to taste
2 sheets phyllo pastry
Olive oil
8 basil leaves

Method
Preheat oven to 350°F (175°C).
Melt butter in a small frying pan. Sweat the spinach and white onion over low heat. Set aside.
Dry-fry the pine nuts in a frying pan. Set aside.
In a bowl, combine spinach, white onion, pine nuts, ricotta, apricots, salt and pepper.
Brush a phyllo pastry sheet with olive oil and cover with the second phyllo pastry sheet.
Cut the pastry into 2" X 13" (5 cm x 33 cm) strips.
Place a basil leaf at the bottom the strip. Top with 1 tbsp (15 mL) of filling.
Take the right corner of the strip and fold over the left corner to make a triangle. Fold the triangle again on the right side of the strip, then the left side of the strip. Repeat (from right to left) until you reach the end of the pastry strip.
Seal the end of the pastry with a little olive oil. Repeat the process with a new strip until there is no more filling left.
Bake the triangles for about 10 minutes, until golden brown. Top with happiness sauce and serve.

Wonton Wrapper Version

Cut an 8-inch (20 cm) square wonton wrapper into quarters.
Use the same folding technique, but seal the wrapper
with egg whites.
Fry the triangles in peanut oil for about 2 minutes.

Sauce Ingredients

1/2 cup (125 mL) sugar
1 tbsp (15 mL) water
1/3 cup (85 mL) cider vinegar
1/3 cup (85 mL) red wine

Method

Combine sugar and water in a small saucepan. Dissolve the sugar over
medium heat without stirring (or the mixture will crystallize) until the
liquid slightly caramelizes. Deglaze with cider vinegar and wine and
reduce by half over high heat.

The sauce, coupled with the softness of the ricotta, the pungent taste of pine nuts and the aroma of apricots – which are synonymous with high quality wines – will thrill the palate. Spine-tingling sensations!

An assemblage of Garganega and Trebbiano, such as a Soave from Veneto, Italy

A Muscat dessert wine from Rhodes, Greece

An assemblage of Viognier and Marsanne from the United States

AUSTRALIAN ABORIGINALS LOVED THE APRICOT'S SOFT SKIN AND JUICY FLESH. THE FLESH OF THE FRUIT WAS CRUSHED AND RUBBED ON THEIR PARTNER'S EROGENOUS ZONES.

Spooned Scallops

Vinaigrette Ingredients
2 tbsp (30 mL) olive oil
1 tbsp (15 mL) walnut oil
1/2 lime – juice and zest
2 tbsp (30 mL) mirin*
1 tsp (5 mL) pink pepper, crushed in a mortar
1/2 clementine – juice and zest

Scallop Ingredients
2 large scallops, diced
1/2 fresh mango, peeled and very finely diced the same size
Mujol caviar (optional)
Fleur de sel (French sea salt), to taste

Method
Mix the vinaigrette ingredients.
One hour before serving, add the scallops and mango to the vinaigrette.
Place into six spoons. Top with caviar and a sprinkle of French sea salt.

* Japanese rice wine, available in supermarkets, Asian grocery stores and
  fine food shops.

This Asian-inspired hors d'oeuvre is a medley of new and exciting flavours. A real feast for the senses. A sturdy white wine is a requisite for tickling the taste buds.

A dry white wine – preferably a vintage Gewurztraminer from Alsace, France

A vintage brut champagne, combining strength, subtlety and structure

A Viognier dry white wine... a Condrieu from the Rhône region in France

SCALLOPS ARE
REPUTED FOR
RAISING SEXUAL
HORMONE
LEVELS. THEIR
FLESH IS SOFT
AND PLEASING
TO THE TONGUE.

!

Sexy Bites of Rolled Duck

Ingredients

1 duck breast, approximately 12 oz (350 g)
Salt and pepper, to taste
1 tbsp (15 mL) quatre-épices (four-spice blend)*
2 colourful beets, peeled
1 tbsp (15 mL) butter
3/8 cup (95 mL) mirin**
2 tbsp (30 mL) honey
3/8 cup (95 mL) rice vinegar
Salt and pepper, to taste
1 green onion, tops only, thinly sliced

EVEN THOUGH BEETS MAY NOT LOOK VERY SUGGESTIVE, THEY SEEM TO BE THE NEW SECRET TO VITALITY. THEY INFLUENCE THE PRODUCTION OF SEXUAL HORMONES.

Method

Score the skin of the duck breast in a criss cross pattern.
Combine salt, pepper and four-spice blend in a dish. Coat duck breast with these spices.
In a very hot ungreased frying pan, sear the duck breast, fat side down, for 3 minutes.
Turn over and continue cooking for 3 minutes. Drain excess fat. Set duck breast aside.
While duck is resting (5 minutes), cut beets into very thin strips.
Melt butter in a saucepan over medium heat. Add beets, mirin, honey, rice vinegar, salt and pepper.
Simmer the mixture until beets are tender and liquid has evaporated, about 5 minutes.
One minute before cooking is complete, add green onion tops and set aside.
Cut duck breast into thin slices. Top with a few beet strips and roll. Secure with a toothpick.

* Quatre-épices (four-spice blend) consists of pepper, clove, nutmeg and ginger.
  It is available in supermarkets.

** Japanese rice wine, available in supermarkets, Asian grocery stores and fine food shops.

The Grenache grape variety, (Garnacha in Spanish), goes well with the mix of spices in this recipe, harmoniously supporting the flavours of the four-spice blend. A delicious, sunny wine is the perfect accompaniment to this succulent and aromatic bird.

A Garnacha from Toro or Ribera del Duero, Spain

A Grenache from the Hérault region in southern France

A Cannonau from the island of Sardinia, Italy

Oyster and Strawberry Fizz

Ingredients
6 oysters
1 cup (250 mL) chopped fresh strawberries
1/2 lime – juice and zest
2 tbsp (30 mL) mirin*
Ground long pepper, to taste
Carbonated water, sparkling wine or champagne

Method
Shuck the oysters. Pour them and their liquid into six shooter glasses.
Put strawberries, lime juice and zest, mirin and long pepper in a blender. Blend until smooth and frothy.
Fill shooter glasses 3/4 full with the juice.
Top with carbonated water, sparkling wine or champagne.

* Japanese rice wine, available in supermarkets, Asian grocery stores and fine food shops.

A SYMBOL OF VENUS, THE GODDESS OF LOVE, STRAWBERRIES ARE JUICY, SWEET, RED AND HEART SHAPED. OYSTERS EVOKE PASSION. THEY ARE LOADED WITH ZINC, WHICH STIMULATES THE PRODUCTION OF TESTOSTERONE. WHAT A COMBINATION!

Honey Nuts

Ingredients
1/4 cup (65 mL) honey or maple syrup
1 tsp (5 mL) butter
1 cup (250 mL) mixed nuts (almonds, pecans, walnuts, hazelnuts)
Fleur de sel (French sea salt), to taste

Method
Preheat oven to 375°C (190°C).
Mix honey and butter. Melt mixture in the microwave for 30 seconds.
Add mixed nuts to the hot mixture.
Line a baking sheet with parchment paper.
Pour mixture on baking sheet and spread nuts out evenly.
Bake for about 20 minutes. Turn nuts over halfway through baking.
Remove from oven and sprinkle with French sea salt.
Let nuts cool for 20 minutes at room temperature.

Variation
Popcorn can be substituted for the mixed nuts.
Bake for 7 minutes.

IN SOME COUNTRIES, NUTS ARE THE SYMBOL OF FERTILITY. HONEY IS THE MOST SEDUCTIVE OF ALL NECTARS. AND MAPLE SYRUP'S GOLDEN LIQUID IS SWEET AND IRRESISTIBLE. TOGETHER, THEY MAKE A DECADENT COMBINATION!

The honey, a most divine nectar, contributes to a sweet mouthfeel and the nuts bring out the bitter notes, which are carried to the long finish. This pairing will soon have you succumbing to the charms of your Aphrodite or Eros.

A nice Italian wine – a Vin Santo from Tuscany

An amontillado sherry from Andalusia, Spain

An aged rum (rhum agricole) from Martinique

As I would free the white almond from the green husk
So would I strip your trappings off,
Beloved.
And fingering the smooth and polished kernel
I should see that in my hands glittered a gem beyond counting.

Amy Lowell (1874-1925)

Sinful Chicken Liver Mousse

Ingredients

1 cup (250 mL) apple juice
7 oz (200 g) chicken livers, trimmed and cut into pieces
1/4 cup (65 mL) dried cranberries
3/8 cup (95 mL) 35% cream or whipping cream
Salt and pepper, to taste
1 tsp (5 mL) ground cardamom
3 tbsp (45 mL) butter, softened
1/4 cup (65 mL) pistachios

Method

Simmer apple juice in a saucepan. Add chicken livers and cover.
Poach chicken livers over medium heat for about 5 minutes. Remove from heat.
Remove chicken livers and pat dry with a paper towel. Set aside.
Add dried cranberries to the cooking juices from the chicken livers.
Let stand for 5 minutes, then drain.
Transfer chicken livers to a food processor. Add ingredients in the following order:
cream, salt, pepper, cardamom and butter.
Puree until smooth.
Put mixture in a bowl. Stir in pistachios and dried cranberries.
Transfer the mixture to a sheet of plastic wrap and roll into a log. Refrigerate for 3 hours.
(The mixture can also be packed into ramekins).
Unwrap the roll and cut into slices.
Serve with brioche (or any type of egg bread)
or baguette/French bread.

This delectable and velvety smooth hors d'oeuvre requires an intimate partner. A perfectly balanced white wine, fat on the finish, is the perfect match for titillating the senses.

A Quart de Chaumes or a Coteaux du Layon from France's Loire Valley region

A high-calibre dry white wine, such as a Meursault, from Côte-d'Or in Burgundy, France

A lightly fortified wine made from Muscat grapes from Veneto, Italy

For the adventurer, a refreshing light pale ale with a lime wedge is sensual company. The fervent aromas of the guacamole's mint or coriander will fire up your imagination and take you to luxurious places filled with fantasy.

A light pale ale, reminiscent of the tropics +⚲⚤

A New Zealand Sauvignon Blanc ♂

A white tequila +⚲⚥

THE AVOCADO HAS LONG BEEN CONSIDERED AN APHRODISIAC. AVOCADOS DANGLE IN PAIRS FROM THE TREE, RESEMBLING TESTICLES. ARABS MADE A PASTE WITH CRUSHED CUMIN SEEDS, WHICH WAS CONSIDERED A STIMULANT... ESPECIALLY FOR WOMEN! OLÉ!

Guacamole Olé Olé!

Ingredients
1 very ripe avocado
1 tbsp (15 mL) lemon juice
Fresh coriander or mint leaves, to taste, finely chopped
A pinch of ground cumin
1 tbsp (15 mL) carbonated water
4 drops Tabasco® sauce
Salt and pepper, to taste

Method
In a bowl, mix all ingredients with a fork or by hand. Serve with tortilla chips.

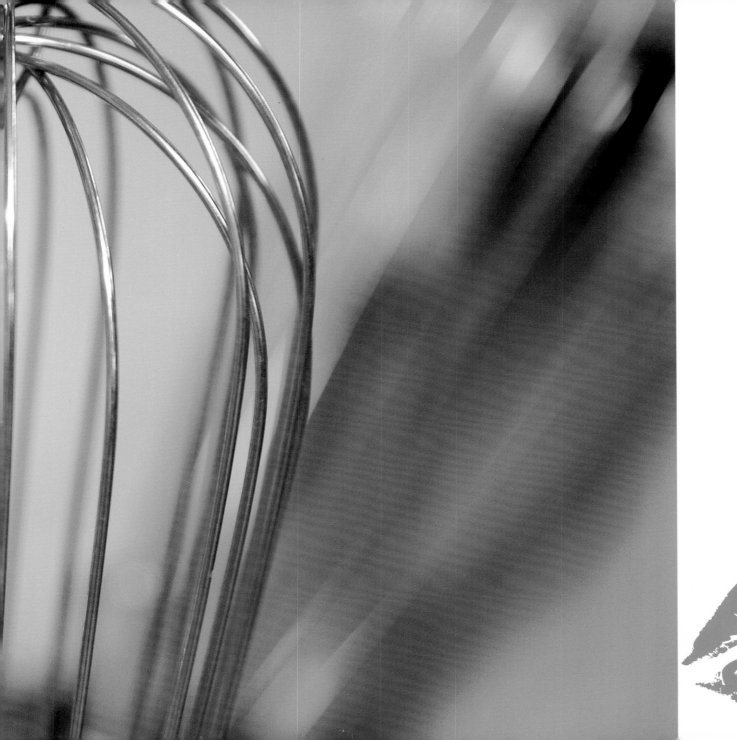

Starters

IT IS SAID THAT
CARDAMOM HAS
STIMULATING
PROPERTIES. IT IS
THE IDEAL BREATH
FRESHENER
AFTER A MEAL, IN
PREPARATION FOR
THINGS TO COME...

Velvety Coconut Soup

Ingredients

1/2 butternut squash [21 oz (600 g)]
2 tbsp (30 mL) olive oil
3 garlic cloves
1 medium onion, diced
1 tbsp (15 mL) fresh ginger, chopped
1 tsp (5 mL) butter
1 apple, peeled and diced
1 cup (250 mL) coconut milk
1-1/2 cups (375 mL) chicken stock
Salt and pepper, to taste
1/2 tsp (2.5 mL) ground cardamom

Method

Preheat oven to 375°F (190°C).
Scoop out the strings and seeds of the butternut squash.
Brush with oil and place garlic inside.
Place butternut squash on a baking sheet and cover with aluminium foil.
Bake for 20-25 minutes until very tender. Set aside.
Meanwhile, in a saucepan, sauté onion and ginger in butter over medium heat.
Add apple to the mixture and simmer for a few minutes.
Scoop out the cooked flesh of the butternut squash and mash with a fork.
Add to saucepan.
Mix coconut milk and chicken stock. Pour into saucepan.
Season with salt, pepper and cardamom.
Simmer soup for about 15 minutes.

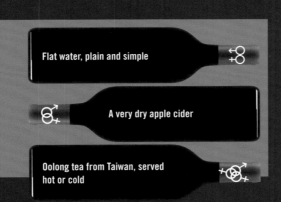

Here, we are in pursuit of both aroma and taste. The texture of the soup cleanses the palate and prepares the taste buds for the delectable apple cider. And in a parade of contrasting textures, tea served cold in a shooter glass intensifies the smooth, buttery texture of the coconut.

Flat water, plain and simple

A very dry apple cider

Oolong tea from Taiwan, served hot or cold

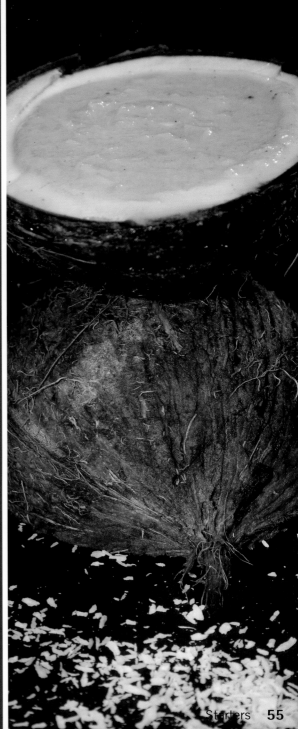

Fantasy of Marrow

Ingredients

4 to 6 beef marrow bones
Fleur de sel (French sea salt)
Fresh chives, snipped
Baguette/French bread

Method

Preheat oven to 450°F (230°C).
Place marrow bones on a baking sheet.
Bake for about 20 minutes.
Watch the cooking time carefully: do not overcook bones or the marrow
will liquefy. Check if cooked by inserting a knife in the marrow and gently
testing the heat of the blade on your lips.
Serve on a wooden plank. Sprinkle with French sea salt and chives. Serve
with baguette/French bread.

Marrow! What a sensual delight… down to the very bone. The fat and soft textures of this dish require a suitable accompaniment: a wine with a racy structure that can stand up to the marrow and will leave you begging for more, again and again.

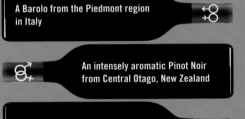

A Barolo from the Piedmont region in Italy

An intensely aromatic Pinot Noir from Central Otago, New Zealand

A Pinot Noir from the Russian River Valley in Sonoma County, USA

Rolled Crab Frenzy

Roll Ingredients

1/4 English cucumber
1/2 carrot
1/4 mango
1/4 red pepper
6 fresh mint leaves
2 green onions
1 tbsp (15 mL) mirin*
1 tbsp (15 mL) rice vinegar
Salt and pepper, to taste
4 rice paper sheets
1 tbsp (15 mL) black sesame seeds
A handful of baby arugula
3.5 oz (100 g) crab meat

Method

Cut cucumber, carrot, mango and red pepper into long thin strips.
Transfer to a medium-sized bowl.
Chop mint leaves and green onion tops. Stir into fruit
and vegetables.
Add mirin and rice vinegar to the above mixture. Season to taste
and mix well.
Dip one rice paper sheet at a time into warm water. Drain on a
paper towel.
Place one rice paper sheet on a work surface. Top with black
sesame seeds, baby arugula, crab meat and mixture. Roll tightly
into a log.

Repeat process with three more rice paper sheets. Slice the four
rolls into bite-sized pieces. Arrange neatly on a serving dish.

Sauce Ingredients

3/8 cup (95 mL) water
2 tbsp (30 mL) fish sauce**
1 tbsp (15 mL) lime juice
1 tbsp (15 mL) sugar
2 tbsp (30 mL) sweet chili sauce

Method

Mix all ingredients in a small bowl. Transfer the sauce to a small
serving bowl and serve with the rolls.

* Japanese rice wine, available in supermarkets, Asian grocery stores
  and fine food shops.

** A very salty and aromatic liquid condiment, made from salted
   fermented fish, and used in Asian cuisine as a substitute for salt.
   In Vietnam it is called nuoc mam, in Thailand nam pla and in Japan
   shottsuru. It is available in supermarkets.

Crab meat's delicate texture is a pleasant match with this medley of fresh fruit and vegetables. A
harmonious and unpretentious wine will be appreciated, glass after glass. So get in a Friday night
state of mind and take it easy… slow and easy!

A dry white Muscadet from France's
Loire Valley region

A Canadian Riesling from the
Niagara Peninsula

A Crémant from Alsace, France

A successful pairing with beef is often linked to the affinity of textures with the wine. The meat's proteins and fat mellow the tannins, giving the wine its excellent taste. Served as a tartare, the beef goes well with a wonderfully fragrant red wine with an exuberant nose and silky tannins. A light and fruity red wine will also do the trick. However, with Parmigiano-Reggiano as an accompaniment, a fragrant white wine is the secret to revealing its charms. Full bodied red wines with strong tannins are not suitable.

An Anjou or Touraine Cabernet Franc from France's Loire Valley region, such as a Bourgueil or a Chinon

A Dolcetto d'Alba from the Piedmont region in Italy

A white wine – a single-varietal Gewurztraminer

ARUGULA BOOSTS SEXUAL ENERGY DUE TO ITS ABUNDANCE OF INVIGORATING AND STIMULATING PROPERTIES. IN THE 12TH CENTURY, ABBESS HILDEGARD OF BINGEN, PHYSICIAN AND HERBALIST, BELIEVED THAT ARUGULA WAS A LOVE POTION AND FORBADE ITS CONSUMPTION TO HER FELLOW NUNS.

Fresh Beefy Nibble

Ingredients
7 oz (200 g) beef tenderloin
Salt, to taste
1 tbsp (15 mL) crushed green peppercorns
1 tbsp (15 mL) butter
1 tbsp (15 mL) olive oil
Truffle oil, to taste
Fleur de sel (French sea salt)
1 oz (28.5 g) Parmigiano-Reggiano shavings
3.5 oz (100 g) baby arugula

Method
Salt the beef tenderloin and roll in crushed green peppercorns.
Sear tenderloin in butter and olive oil for 30 seconds per side.
Allow tenderloin to cool in the fridge. Cut into thin slices.
Spread out beef slices on a chilled serving dish.
Drizzle with truffle oil and sprinkle with French sea salt.
Garnish with Parmigiano-Reggiano shavings.
Serve with baby arugula.

Oh! Tender skin
Oh! Irresistible flesh
Let us start fresh
Until we win
Let us begin
Until we sin

Erotica

Decadent Cocoa Foie Gras

Foie Gras Ingredients
7 oz (200 g) foie gras, deveined
Salt, to taste
1 tbsp (15 mL) cocoa powder butter*
1 tbsp (15 mL) cocoa powder
Pepper, to taste

Method
Preheat oven to 400°F (205°C).
Cut foie gras in half. Season each piece with salt on both sides.
Mix cocoa butter powder and cocoa powder. Dip foie gras in mixture to coat.
In a large preheated frying pan, sear the foie gras over high heat for about
30 seconds on each side.
Transfer foie gras to a baking sheet and bake for 5 minutes.
Place foie gras on a paper towel to absorb excess fat. Season with pepper.

Cherry Sauce Ingredients
1 tsp (5 mL) butter
1 grey shallot, finely chopped
1/2 cup (125 mL) black cherries, frozen
1 tbsp (15 mL) sugar
Salt and pepper, to taste

Method
Melt butter in a pan over medium heat. Sauté shallot until tender.
Add black cherries and simmer for a few minutes.
Add sugar, then salt and pepper to taste. Continue cooking for 2 or 3 minutes.

Serve foie gras with cherry sauce and grilled bread.

* Cocoa butter powder prevents the foie gras from melting too fast. This light yellow
  powder is available in chocolate shops.

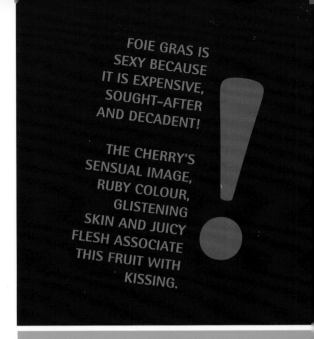

FOIE GRAS IS SEXY BECAUSE IT IS EXPENSIVE, SOUGHT-AFTER AND DECADENT!

THE CHERRY'S SENSUAL IMAGE, RUBY COLOUR, GLISTENING SKIN AND JUICY FLESH ASSOCIATE THIS FRUIT WITH KISSING.

Appetizing, seductive, provocative and exciting, foie gras prepared this way calls out for a red wine to bring out its virtues. After all, an evening like this is about taking full advantage of the delectable things life has to offer. Bottoms up!

A sweet fortified wine – a Maury from the Roussillon region in France

A 10 year – or better yet – 20 year old Tawny Port

A Sauternes or Barsac dessert wine from Bordeaux, France

Audacious Egg Salad

Salad Ingredients

4 fingerling potatoes
14 oz (400 g) green beans
4 quail eggs
4 cherry tomatoes, cut in half
6 black olives, pits removed
A handful of baby chicory

Method

Cook potatoes in salted water, drain and set aside.
Blanch green beans in salted boiling water. Drain and rinse with cold water. Set aside.
Hard boil quail eggs in water and a bit of vinegar for 4 minutes. Rinse under cold water. Remove shell and cut in half. Set aside.
Prepare the vinaigrette while vegetables and eggs are cooking (see recipe).

Vinaigrette is wine's worst enemy. Its acidity can ruin all the qualities of a good wine. But the mustard and yogurt used to bind the vinaigrette make up for this by reducing the acidity. Here, a wine pairing is consequential and therefore bold!

Flat water... a safe bet

A dry white wine, fragrant and low in acid, with notes of iodine, such as a Chablis from Burgundy, France

A rosé from Provence, France

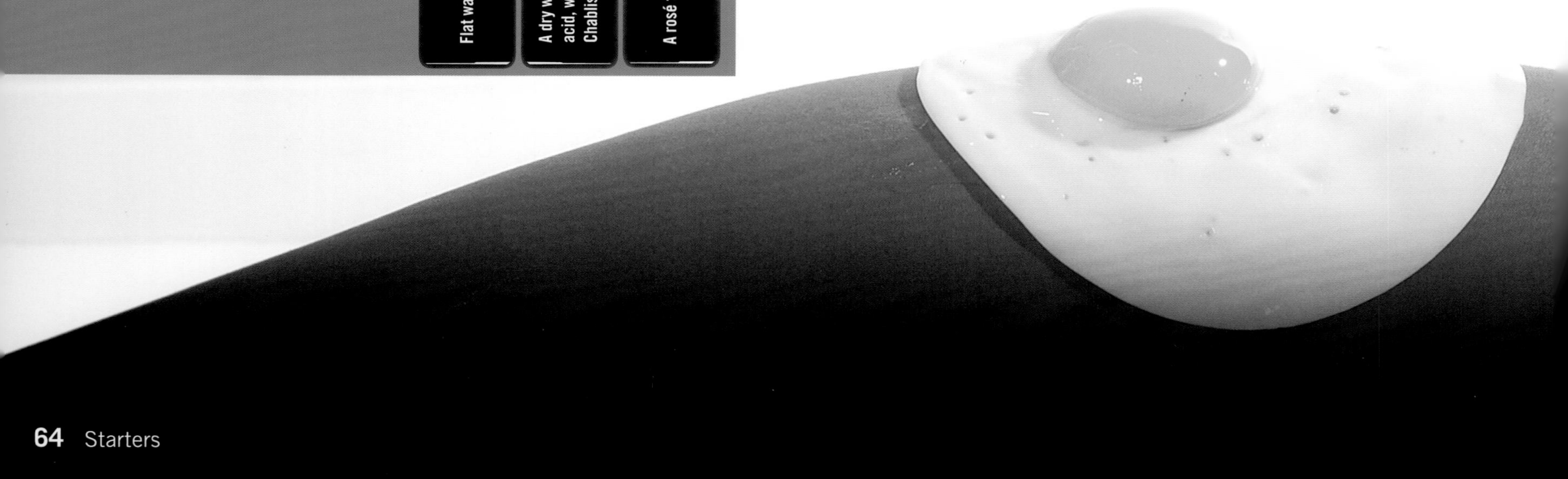

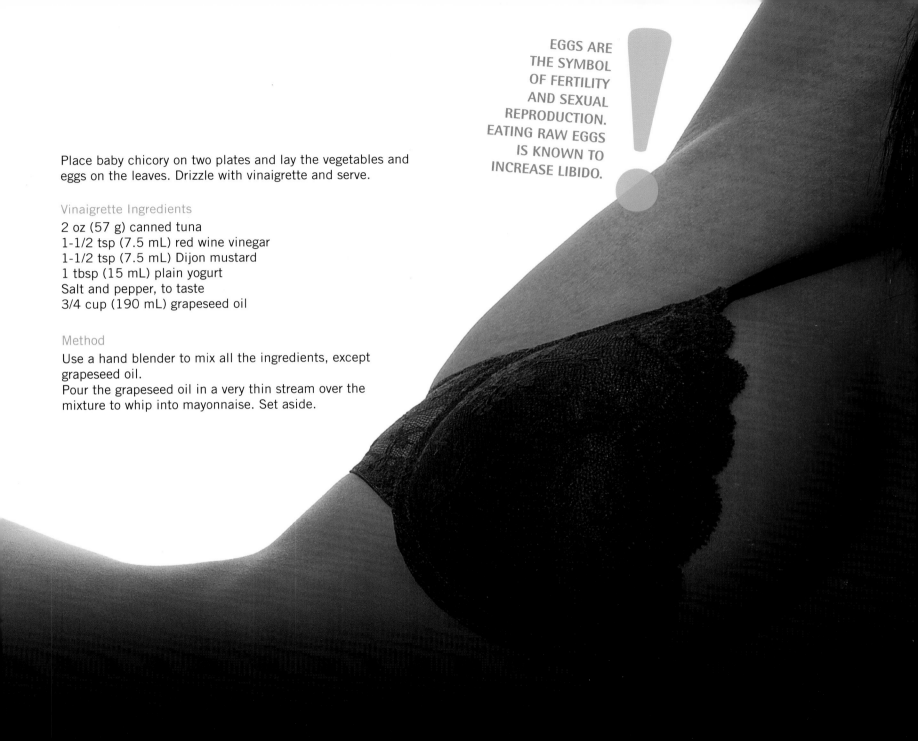

Place baby chicory on two plates and lay the vegetables and eggs on the leaves. Drizzle with vinaigrette and serve.

Vinaigrette Ingredients

2 oz (57 g) canned tuna
1-1/2 tsp (7.5 mL) red wine vinegar
1-1/2 tsp (7.5 mL) Dijon mustard
1 tbsp (15 mL) plain yogurt
Salt and pepper, to taste
3/4 cup (190 mL) grapeseed oil

Method

Use a hand blender to mix all the ingredients, except grapeseed oil.
Pour the grapeseed oil in a very thin stream over the mixture to whip into mayonnaise. Set aside.

EGGS ARE THE SYMBOL OF FERTILITY AND SEXUAL REPRODUCTION. EATING RAW EGGS IS KNOWN TO INCREASE LIBIDO.

Celebrate this orgy
Of uncontrolled indulgence
Reunion of extreme foodies
Men and women in mergence
Wine please!
Love has no patience!

Erotica

This orgiastic jumble of fried squid, with its hot and spicy flavours, is a journey into the Mediterranean. Bring on the orgy... it's about time! Festive wines are definitely right for the occasion.

A white sparkling wine, such as a Brut Reserva Cava from Catalonia, Spain

A Tavel rosé from the Rhône region in France

A Patrimonio, a Vermentino dry white wine from Corsica, France

Calamari Orgy

Sauce Ingredients
4 tbsp (60 mL) orange marmalade
1/2 tsp (2.5 mL) prepared horseradish
1 tbsp (15 mL) water
Salt and pepper, to taste

Method
Mix all ingredients in a small bowl. Set aside.

Calamari Ingredients
4 or 5 calamari, cleaned [10.5 oz (300 g)]
6 drops Tabasco® sauce
1/2 cup (125 mL) all-purpose flour
1/2 cup (125 mL) rice flour
Salt and pepper, to taste
1 tsp (5 mL) paprika
Peanut oil, as needed

Method
Cut calamari into 1/2-inch (1 cm) rings.
Place calamari in a bowl and add 6 drops Tabasco sauce. Mix well.
Mix all-purpose flour, rice flour, salt, pepper and paprika in a medium-sized bowl.
Dip calamari in the flour mixture to coat them. Shake off excess flour.
Heat peanut oil in a large saucepan.
Fry the calamari in peanut oil for about one minute. Serve with the sauce.

HORSERADISH PULP IS SAID TO HAVE APHRODISIAC PROPERTIES. EARLY GREEKS USED THE HERB AS A BACK RUB AND APHRODISIAC.

!

Mushroom Escargot Kiss

Ingredients
A pinch of saffron
1/4 cup (65 mL) dry white wine
2 large portobello mushrooms
Olive oil, as needed
4 slices mild pancetta
16 medium escargots, rinsed and drained
1 garlic clove, finely chopped
Pepper, to taste
1/2 cup (125 mL) 35% cream or whipping cream
1 green onion, chopped

Method
Preheat oven to 350°F (175°C).
Soak saffron in white wine.
Gently remove the stems from the portobello mushrooms. Using a spoon, carefully remove the dark gills from the underside of the caps.
Brush mushrooms with olive oil. Bake for 5 minutes. Set aside.
In a frying pan, sauté pancetta in a little olive oil. Drain excess fat.
Add escargots and garlic to pancetta. Fry for 1 minute.
Deglaze with white wine. Season mixture with pepper.
Add cream and reduce for 3 minutes.
Add green onion to the mixture just before serving.
Fill one mushroom cap with the mixture and cover with the second.
For two people to share!

The portobello mushrooms and escargots, as well as the creamy filling, bring out the exquisite flavours of the saffron and pancetta, which are the heart of this delicious recipe. The dish requires a white wine that can back up such a tasty combination.

A slightly woody California Chardonnay

A Canadian Chardonnay from The Bench in the Niagara Peninsula

A Riesling from Alsace, France will thrill the taste buds to no end!

Essentials

Frisky Rabbit Confit

Rabbit Confit Ingredients
2 rabbit legs, 8 oz (225 g) each
4 cups (1 L) duck fat

Dry Marinade Ingredients
1 tsp (5 mL) quatre-épices (four-spice blend)*
2 tbsp (30 mL) brown sugar
1 garlic clove, finely chopped
1/4 cup (65 mL) coarse salt

Method
Preheat oven to 300°F (150°C).
Place rabbit legs on a baking sheet, skin side down.
Combine all the ingredients of the dry marinade. Press firmly to coat rabbit legs.

NUTMEG DILATES THE BLOOD VESSELS AND RAISES BODY TEMPERATURE; PEPPER STIMULATES THE SENSES; CLOVES ARE CONSIDERED ONE OF THE MOST POTENT NATURAL APHRODISIACS; AND GINGER FACILITATES ERECTIONS AND INCREASES WOMEN'S SEX DRIVE. HOORAY FOR THE FOUR-SPICE BLEND!

The rabbit's spicy notes from the marinade and slow cooking in duck fat bring soft and sweet sensations to the mouth, like a French kiss.

Wines from Tempranillo, Mourvèdre or Tannat grapes go remarkably well with this meal, and there are several excellent ones all over the world. The confit style of cooking summons the high quality, well balanced Syrah wines of the appellations from France's northern Rhône region.

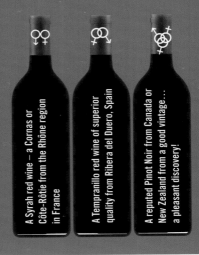

A Syrah red wine – a Cornas or Côte-Rôtie from the Rhône region in France

A Tempranillo red wine of superior quality from Ribera del Duero, Spain

A reputed Pinot Noir from Canada or New Zealand from a good vintage… a pleasant discovery!

Cover with plastic wrap and refrigerate for 24 hours.
Wipe off dry marinade from the rabbit legs with a wet paper towel.
Melt duck fat in an ovenproof dish over medium heat.
Place rabbit legs in melted duck fat. Cover and bake for about 2 hours.
Remove rabbit legs from oven. Drain off fat. Set aside. When ready to serve, preheat broiler. Broil rabbit legs for about 5 minutes.

Serve rabbit confit with a delicious cauliflower celeriac puree (see recipe).

*   Quatre-épices (four-spice blend) consists of pepper, clove, nutmeg and ginger. It is available in supermarkets.

Cauliflower Celeriac Puree

Ingredients
1/2 cauliflower [9 oz (260 g)]
1/2 celeriac [8 oz (230 g)]
1/2 fennel [7 oz (200 g)]
1/4 cup (65 mL) 35% cream or whipping cream
4 tbsp (60 mL) butter
Salt and pepper, to taste

Method
Cut vegetables into pieces. Boil in salted boiling water until very tender.
Drain well. Place vegetables in a blender.
Add cream, butter, salt and pepper. Puree until smooth and creamy.

Lamb calls out for structured wines with an elegant mouthfeel. So very well balanced! Wine lovers know this, as they have already tasted it. Novices will be won over. No more words. Chills up and down the spine and an orgasm on the palate. More, please!

A highly reputed Pauillac — for those with deep pockets — or a Moulis Cru Bourgeois from Bordeaux, France

A red wine — a superior vin de pays from Hérault in France's Languedoc-Roussillon region.

A "Super Tuscan" from Italy

FENNEL CONTAINS ESTROGEN AND INCREASES SEX DRIVE.

Carnal Pleasure Lamb Shanks

Ingredients

2 lamb shanks
1 garlic clove, finely chopped
2 tbsp (30 mL) fresh mint, chopped
1 tsp (5 mL) olive oil
1/4 cup (65 mL) flour
Olive oil, as needed
1 medium onion, chopped
1/2 fennel, diced [5 oz (140 g)]
1/2 celeriac, diced [8 oz (230 g)]
1-1/2 cups (375 mL) chicken stock
Salt, to taste
Ground pepper, to taste
7 to 10 mint leaves

Method

Preheat oven to 300°F (150°C).
Make 4 or 5 incisions in each lamb shank.
Mix garlic, fresh mint and olive oil. Insert mixture into each incision.
Cover lamb shanks in plastic wrap and refrigerate for 3 hours.
Dust lamb shanks with flour. Heat a bit of olive oil in a cast iron pot or Dutch oven set over high heat. Sear shanks on both sides.
Remove from pot and set aside.
In the same pot, add a bit of olive oil and sauté onion, fennel and celeriac for a few minutes until brown.
Add chicken stock, salt and pepper.
Return lamb shanks to pot. Cover with lid and place in the oven.
Braise for 1-1/2 to 2 hours or until lamb is very tender.
Top with mint leaves.

Serve with root vegetables, such as baby turnips, carrots or parsnips.

The convergence of Mediterranean aromas and flavours is always enticing to the taste buds. A sunny white wine with a strong acidic backbone is the perfect match for this sensual rendezvous.

A Sauvignon Blanc from Pessac-Léognan in Bordeaux, France

Another Sauvignon Blanc from Sancerre in France's Loire Valley region

A Sauvignon Blanc from California, USA

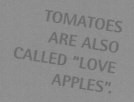

TOMATOES ARE ALSO CALLED "LOVE APPLES".

Saucy Mussels with Tomatoes

Ingredients
Mussels, 3 to 4 lb (1.3 to 1.8 kg)
2 tbsp (30 mL) olive oil
2 garlic cloves, chopped
1 onion, chopped
1/4 cup (65 mL) dry red wine
2 cups (500 mL) diced tomatoes, in juice
2 pinches crushed chili peppers
Salt and pepper, to taste
Chopped fresh parsley, to taste

Method
Clean and debeard mussels under cold water.
In a large cooking pot, sauté garlic and onion in olive oil for a few minutes until brown.
Add red wine and simmer for 3 minutes.
Add tomatoes and their juice, as well as crushed chili peppers, salt and pepper. Simmer sauce for about 20 minutes.
Use a hand blender to blend the sauce until smooth.
Remove half of the sauce. Set aside and keep warm.
Add mussels to the remaining sauce in the cooking pot.
Cover and simmer over medium-high heat for 5 minutes. Mussels are ready when they pop open.
Remove mussels from heat and transfer to a large bowl. Pour remaining sauce over mussels and sprinkle with chopped parsley.

Sultry Bucatini with Clams

Flavours redolent of the sea, acidity from the tomato and the spiciness of chili peppers... this combination requires a pairing that is flexible so that each ingredient can thrive next to the other. The wine can also be sharp, bold and sassy depending on the mood.

A woody white wine – a Chardonnay from the Alto Adige region in northern Italy

A California Chardonnay Reserve of exceptional distinction

A red wine... a decanted Valpolicella Ripasso from Veneto, Italy

CLAMS ARE EVOCATIVE BECAUSE THEY RESEMBLE WOMEN'S GENITALS. THEY ARE HIGH IN ZINC, WHICH IMPROVES SEXUAL POTENCY.

Ingredients

2 tbsp (30 mL) olive oil
1 cup (250 mL) leek (white portion only), finely sliced
1 garlic clove, finely chopped
1 cup (250 mL) frozen peas
5 cherry tomatoes, cut in half
A pinch of crushed chili peppers
1 can Stimpson's surf clams* or common clams [5 oz (142 g)]
1/2 cup (125 mL) fish stock
Salt, to taste
1 tbsp (15 mL) butter
8 oz (225 g) bucatini pasta**
10 fresh clams, scrubbed (optional)

Method

Bring a large pot of salted water to a boil. Cook bucatini al dente.
Drain and rinse.
Meanwhile, heat olive oil in a large frying pan over medium heat.
Sweat leek and garlic.
Add peas and tomatoes to the pan. Cook for a few minutes.
Add crushed chili peppers, clam liquid from the can (set clams aside)
and fish stock. Bring to a boil. Reduce heat and simmer for 3 to 4 minutes.
Add canned clams. Season with salt and add butter.
Pour sauce over bucatini pasta.

Add a few fresh clams to complement the dish. Bring 1 cup (250 mL) white wine to a boil in a small saucepan. Add clams – they will pop open in less than 5 minutes!

* The Stimpson's surf clam is found in the St Lawrence River along the North Shore of Quebec. This bivalve mollusc is much larger than the common clam. It is available is most fish stores and some fine food shops.

** Bucatini pasta is the same length as spaghetti but larger in diameter, with a thin hole down the center.

Virile Lobster

Lobster Ingredients
2 lobsters, 1-3/4 lb (800 g) each
Salted water*, enough to cover lobsters

Method
Bring large pot of salted water to a boil and plunge lobsters headfirst. Calculate cooking time when water starts boiling again. Cook lobsters according to the recommended cooking times (see chart).
Cut the lobsters in half lengthwise and twist off claws.
Serve warm.

Sauce Ingredients
1 to 2 garlic cloves, to taste
1 egg yolk
1/2 lemon, juice only
Salt and pepper, to taste
1/2 cup (125 mL) olive oil

Method
Crush garlic in a mortar. Transfer to a small bowl.
Add egg yolk, lemon juice, salt and pepper. Mix well.
Pour a thin stream of olive oil on the mixture and whisk into a smooth sauce.

Serve sauce as an accompaniment to the lobsters. Quick, easy and delicious!

* 1 tbsp (15 mL) salt per 4 cups (1 L) water.

LOBSTER COOKING TIMES		
Weight	Cooking Times (minutes)	
	Male	Female
3/4 lb (340 g)	8	10
1 to 1-1/4 lb (450 g to 565 g)	10	12
1-1/2 lb (680 g)	14	16
2 lb (900 g)	16	20
3 lb (1.35 kg)	18	23

The intense oral contact with the lobster meat covered in a smooth sauce, with an accompanying wine worthy of these flavours, makes this union a delicious obsession with climactic results.

A dry white wine – a Pinot Gris from Alsace (Grand Cru), France

A white wine – a Viura from Rioja, Spain

A Vin Jaune (yellow wine) made from Savagnin grapes from Jura, France

Seductive Duck Breast with Molasses

Ingredients
1 duck breast, 1 lb (450 g)
1 tbsp (15 mL) dry red wine
1/4 cup (65 mL) molasses
Ground Sichuan pepper, to taste
Salt, to taste

Method
Preheat oven to 375°F (190°C).
Mix wine, molasses, Sichuan pepper and salt. Heat in a small saucepan for a few minutes. Set glaze aside and keep warm.
Score the skin of the duck breast in a criss cross pattern.
In an ovenproof pan, sear the duck breast on high heat, fat side down, for 2 minutes.
Turn over and cook for 2 more minutes.
Drain excess fat. Brush duck breast with a bit of glaze. Bake for about 8 minutes until rare.
Remove duck breast from oven. Rest for 5 minutes to allow juices to settle in the meat.
Cut duck breast into 3/4-inch (2 cm) slices and coat with glaze.

Serve with Jerusalem artichokes sautéed in butter.

This plump and voluptuous duck breast will tempt you with its labyrinth of flavours where the meat and glaze come together. The wine must be able to back this union with finesse.

A Madiran red wine from South West France

A Syrah – a Côte-Rôtie or Hermitage from the Rhône region in France

A high calibre Australian Shiraz

With white meat, blue cheese and cream, you would select a white wine, no questions asked. Granted, but what about the tomatoes? A supple and fruity red wine would be better than a white wine, but not just any!

A red wine from northern Italy, such as a Nebbiolo d'Alba

A Zinfandel from California, USA

A nicely crafted dry white wine from the Rhône region in France

Undress me
One layer at a time
Taste me slowly
Until my heart you find

Erotica

Paramour Veal with Blue Cheese

Ingredients
2 bone-in veal chops, 10 oz (285 g) each
Salt and pepper, to taste
3 tbsp (45 mL) blue cheese
1/3 cup (85 mL) dry white wine
2/3 cup (170 mL) 35% cream or whipping cream
4 sun-dried tomatoes, diced

Method
Season veal chops with salt and pepper.
Pan-fry veal for 5 minutes per side. Meat should be
pink in the centre.
Meanwhile, mix blue cheese and wine in a saucepan.
Whisk mixture over low heat until blue cheese melts.
Add cream and sun-dried tomatoes. Reduce sauce
to a creamy consistency.

Spoon sauce over veal chops. Serve with fresh
artichoke (or canned artichoke hearts that have been
heated in the sauce), green salad and baked potato.

Tuna Threesome

Mango Marmalade Ingredients
1 mango
1 tbsp (15 mL) olive oil
3 tbsp (45 mL) ginger, very finely diced the same size
3 tbsp (45 mL) sugar
1/2 cup (125 mL) water
Salt and pepper, to taste

Tuna Ingredients
2 tuna steaks, 150g (5oz) each
1 tbsp (15 mL) butter
1 tbsp (15 mL) olive oil
Gomasio*, enough to coat the tuna
3 oz (100 g) wakame seaweed**

Method
Puree mango and olive oil in a blender. Set aside.
Mix ginger, sugar and water in a pan. Simmer until water
has evaporated.
Add to mango mixture.
Season with salt and pepper. Set aside.
Sear tuna in olive oil and butter over high heat for
2 minutes each side.
Coat tuna steaks with gomasio.
Serve tuna, wakame seaweed and mango marmalade
in three separate serving dishes.

*   A dry condiment made from toasted sesame seeds and sea salt.
     It is available in health food stores.

     Homemade gomasio: Grind 4 tbsp (60 mL) toasted sesame seeds
     with 1 tbsp (15 mL) coarse sea salt.

**   A thin seaweed available in supermarkets or fish stores.

Three possibilities:

The herbaceous flavours of wakame seaweed
and gomasio merit a "Classic" pairing.

The spiciness of ginger and
accompanying flavours is a "Love at First
Taste" match.

The sweetness of mango's fruity
flavour deserves a "Libertine" pairing.

What do we wish to accomplish?
Sultriness, luxury or straight out debauchery?

A dry sparkling wine, such as a
Crémant from Burgundy, France

A Sauvignon Blanc from France's
Bordeaux wine region

A dessert wine from France's Loire
Valley region, such as a Vouvray

IN INDIA, AYURVEDIC
MEDICINE
(NATUROPATHIC
MEDICINE) PRESCRIBES
SESAME TO TREAT
SEXUAL PROBLEMS. IN
COOKING, ITS TOASTED
SEEDS ARE SIMPLY
IRRESISTIBLE!

THE MANGO'S
APPEARANCE, SWEET
JUICY YELLOW FLESH
AND SMOOTH SILKY
TEXTURE MAKE IT A
SYMBOL OF SEXUALITY
IN ASIA.

Veal Sweetbread Satisfaction

Veal sweetbreads are extremely delicate and require careful preparation to bring out their captivating textures. Like love, a few preliminaries are necessary to make way for pleasurable consumption.

A dry white wine – a Meursault from Burgundy, France

A Condrieu white wine from the Rhône region in France

A Champagne magnum – a demi-sec or a blanc de blancs

Veal Sweetbread Ingredients

1-3/4 lb (800 g) veal sweetbreads
5 cups (1.25 mL) court bouillon*
Butter, as needed
1 tbsp (15 mL) olive oil

Method

Bring court bouillon to a boil. Poach veal sweetbreads for 5 minutes.
Rinse under cold water and peel off the membrane.
Melt butter and olive oil in a pan over high heat. Brown the veal sweetbreads, basting frequently with melted butter until crispy. Place veal sweetbreads on a paper towel.

Sauce Ingredients

1 tbsp (15 mL) olive oil
1 tbsp (15 mL) butter
1 leek (white portion only), thinly sliced
1 tsp (5 mL) green peppercorns
1/2 cup (125 mL) dry white wine
1/4 cup (65 mL) apple cider
1/4 cup (65 mL) dry white vermouth
1 tbsp (15 mL) honey
1/2 cup (125 mL) 35% cream or whipping cream
1-1/2 tsp (7.5 mL) fresh tarragon, chopped

Method

In a saucepan, sweat the leeks in butter and olive oil.
Add green peppercorns. Deglaze with white wine, apple cider and vermouth. Simmer for 2 to 3 minutes.
Stir in honey and cream. Simmer until sauce is smooth and creamy.
Add tarragon just before serving.

A simple potato and sweet potato puree is the perfect accompaniment for the veal sweetbreads.

* Court bouillon is a flavoured liquid for poaching foods. Traditionally, court bouillon is water, bay leaves, carrots, celery, onion, parsley and garlic.

Salmon Desire

Ingredients

12 oz (345 g) salmon filet
2 tbsp (30 mL) natural pistachios
1 tbsp (15 mL) fresh dill, snipped
1 tbsp (15 mL) 35% cream or whipping cream
Salt and pepper, to taste
2 tbsp (30 mL) chives, snipped
1 grey shallot, finely chopped
1/2 lemon – juice only
1-1/2 tsp (7.5 mL) walnut oil

Method

Cut the salmon into small cubes.
Coarsely chop pistachios.
Lightly whisk cream.
Mix all ingredients in a bowl.

Serve with finely sliced potatoes that have been brushed with olive oil
and broiled, or simply sea salt potato chips.

Chardonnay and fresh salmon with dill… an indisputable gastronomic match. Here, we are spoiled for choice and the quality on offer is just as varied. Enjoy!

A French white Burgundy, particularly from the Côte de Beaune region

A Canadian Chardonnay from the Niagara Peninsula

An American Chardonnay, particularly from Oregon, as well as Rutherford and Sonoma County in California

Impulse of Venison and Grapes

Venison Ingredients
1 venison steak, 12 oz (350 g)
1 tsp (5 mL) butter
1 tsp (5 mL) olive oil

Sauce Ingredients
1 tsp (5 mL) corn starch
1 tbsp (15 mL) water
1 cup (250 mL) green grapes
1/2 cup (125 mL) frozen blueberries
1/4 cup (65 mL) maple syrup
1/4 cup (65 mL) Port wine
Salt and pepper, to taste

Method
Preheat oven to 400°F (205°C).
In an ovenproof pan, sear venison steak in butter and olive oil on both sides over high heat. Then bake for 8 minutes.
Meanwhile, mix water and corn starch. Set aside.
In a saucepan, bring grapes, blueberries, maple syrup and Port wine to a boil.
Whisk the water and corn starch mixture into the sauce.
Simmer until sauce thickens.
Season with salt and pepper, to taste.
Remove venison from oven. Allow to rest for 5 minutes.

Slice the venison. Top with sauce and serve.

Luxury has a price and your loved one deserves the very finest. In days of yore, venison was reserved for nobles and royals. So it is only appropriate to serve wine fit for a king. Nothing less will do. We have necessities and luxuries but here, these are luxurious necessities. Life's too short…

A red wine – a Châteauneuf-du-Pape from the southern Rhône region in France

A 10 year old Brunello di Montalcino from Tuscany, Italy

Why not enjoy both?

It is in her eyes
She feels the passion
It is between her thighs
She feels no burden
It is with her mouth
She wants to be kissed
She has no doubt
She won't resist

Erotica

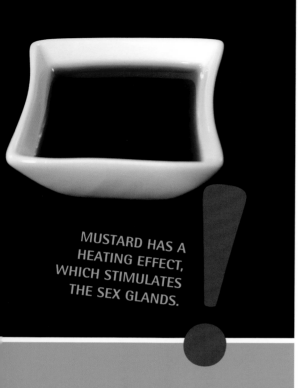

MUSTARD HAS A HEATING EFFECT, WHICH STIMULATES THE SEX GLANDS.

A Cabernet Sauvignon, without a doubt. It's the most fashionable grape variety on the planet. Complex and subtle, this grape produces legendary wines with unique features. At their peak, in the great vintages, the best ones lead to pleasures of the mind and flesh.

A Médoc red wine from Bordeaux, France

A red wine – a Finis Terrae Cabernet Sauvignon from Chile

A Nuits-Saint-Georges from Burgundy, France

Hot Beef Injection

Beef Ingredients

1/2 cup (125 mL) black olives, pits removed
1 garlic clove
12 oz (350 g) filet mignon
Salt and pepper, to taste
1 tbsp (15 mL) butter
1 tbsp (15 mL) whole-grain Meaux mustard
Puff pastry
1 egg yolk
1 tbsp (15 mL) milk

Method

Preheat oven to 400°F (205°C).
Use a chopper to chop up olives and garlic. Set aside.
Season filet mignon with salt and pepper. In a frying pan, sear both sides in butter over high heat.
Remove filet mignon and place on a work surface. Spread Meaux mustard over the filet mignon, pressing the mustard so it adheres well to the meat.
Repeat process with the olive and garlic mixture.
Wrap filet mignon in puff pastry. Place on a baking sheet lined with parchment paper.
Mix egg yolk and milk, and brush over puff pastry.
Place filet mignon in the oven and bake for 30 minutes until meat is pink in the centre.
Allow filet mignon to rest for 10 minutes. Meanwhile, prepare the sauce.

Sauce Ingredients

2 cups (500 mL) brown veal stock
3/8 cup (95 mL) red wine
Salt and pepper, to taste
1 tbsp (15 mL) butter

Method

Mix brown veal stock, red wine, salt and pepper in a small saucepan. Reduce mixture over medium heat to one-third.
Remove from heat and whisk in butter.

Serve with sauce and a tian of grilled vegetables.

Your beautiful legs
Your delicious thighs
They hop and dance
Like no one else
They take me to the skies
Can you see it in my eyes?

Hot Legs

Ingredients

3 tbsp (30 mL) olive oil, in total
3 tbsp (30 mL) butter, in total
1 small onion, chopped
2 garlic cloves, finely chopped
1 large sweet potato, diced [12 oz (350 g)]
Salt and pepper, to taste
6 large chicken drumsticks
1 can black beans [19 oz (540 mL)], rinsed and drained
1 bay leaf
8 green olives
1 tsp (5 mL) curry powder
4 cups (1 L) chicken stock
2 star anise
1 preserved lemon, cut into quarters
4 merguez sausages*
Salt and pepper, to taste

Method

Preheat oven to 350°F (175°C).
In a large saucepan, brown the onion and garlic in 1 tbsp (15 mL) each of olive oil and butter. Transfer to a cast iron pot.
In the saucepan, add 1 tbsp (15 mL) each of olive oil and butter and brown the sweet potato. Transfer to the cast iron pot.
Add remaining olive oil and butter to the same saucepan. Season chicken thighs with salt and pepper. Brown over high heat and transfer to the cast iron pot.
Deglaze the saucepan with chicken stock. Pour into cast iron pot.
Add black beans, bay leaf, green olives, curry powder, star anise, lemon and merguez sausages.
Cover and bake for about 1 hour.
Season with salt and pepper. Serve on a bed of couscous.

* Merguez sausages are thin and spicy. Originating from the Maghreb, they are available almost everywhere.

SWEET POTATOES CONTAIN NUTRIENTS THAT NOURISH THE SEX HORMONES. IN SOUTH AMERICA, SWEET POTATOES ARE USED TO STIMULATE WOMEN'S SEX DRIVE.

Hot thighs and legs, oh my! They captivate the imagination of lovers and gastronomes alike, especially when they are on hand… or better yet, in the mouth!

The tender drumsticks and spicy merguez sausages are sure to spark off your naughty imagination. Paper plates and plastic glasses will have you spending less time washing up and more time getting down…

A Viognier white wine from Pays d'Oc, France

Again, a Viognier white wine – a Condrieu from the Rhône region in France, or Napa Valley, USA

A Pinot Noir, such as a Mercurey from Burgundy, France

Fried fish coated in spicy tempura, served with a fruity, sweet and vanilla-infused accompaniment, begs for a seductive wine. This meal requires an aged wine with enough strength to tame the sambal oelek but, at the same time, is delicate enough to honour the sweet flavours of the peach compote.

A mature white wine, fat in the mouth, with a 14% alcohol content is the perfect partner. However, a red wine could surprise you. Forget water or any type of carbonated drink.

A Chardonnay from Tuscany, Italy

A Reserve Chardonnay from Napa Valley, USA

A red wine – a Pinot Noir aged at least 10 years, from Burgundy or the Loire Valley region in France

Sweet Little Sins of Halibut

Peach Compote Ingredients

4 very ripe peaches
5/8 cup (160 mL) water
2 tbsp (30 mL) brown sugar
1 vanilla bean
Salt and pepper, to taste

Method

Peel peaches and cut into pieces.
Mix all ingredients in a small saucepan and cook over medium heat.
Reduce mixture by three-quarters.
Use a hand blender to puree the mixture. Set aside.

Halibut Ingredients

10.5 oz (300 g) halibut
1 ice cube
3 tbsp (45 mL) cold water
1/2 tsp (2.5 mL) sambal oelek*
Salt and pepper, to taste
1/3 cup (85 mL) tempura batter mix
1 cup (250 mL) panko breadcrumbs**
Peanut oil, as needed

Method

Cut halibut into strips.
In a bowl, make tempura batter by mixing all the ingredients,
except panko breadcrumbs and peanut oil.
Heat peanut oil in a large saucepan or deep fryer.
Dip halibut into the tempura batter. Then dip into panko breadcrumbs.
Fry breaded halibut strips in peanut oil for about 3 minutes.
Serve immediately with peach compote as a dip.

* Sambal oelek is a sauce made with chili peppers. It is available in most supermarkets, Asian grocery stores and fine food shops.

** Panko are coarse, crunchy Japanese breadcrumbs available in supermarkets.

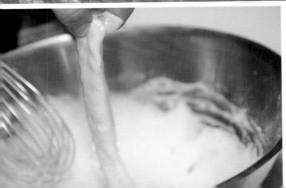

PEANUTS ARE HIGH IN VITAMIN E AND ZINC, WHICH HELP PRODUCE TESTOSTERONE AND INCREASE SEX DRIVE.

The wonderful oriental aromas in this dish will permeate the home and entice the taste buds. A seriously seductive recipe that sets the mood for an equally seductive evening.

A Chardonnay white wine from Oregon, USA

A Savennières white wine from France's Loire Valley region

A Chardonnay white wine from Chile's Central Valley region

Hanky Panky Pork

Pork Tenderloin Ingredients

1 pork tenderloin, 1 lb (450 g)
1 tbsp (15 mL) olive oil
1 tbsp (15 mL) butter
1/4 cup (65 mL) raw peanuts (unroasted, unsalted)

Sauce Ingredients

1/4 cup (65 mL) natural peanut butter
2 tbsp (30 mL) brown sugar
2 tbsp (30 mL) Hoisin sauce*
1-1/2 tsp (7.5 mL) rice vinegar
1-1/2 tsp (7.5 mL) mirin**
1-1/2 tsp (7.5 mL) fish sauce***
1 tbsp (15 mL) soya sauce
1/2 tsp (2.5 mL) sambal oelek***
2 tbsp (30 mL) water

Method

Preheat oven to 375°F (190°C).
In a large ovenproof pan, sear pork tenderloin in olive oil and butter on both sides. Then bake for 20 minutes. Remove pork tenderloin from the oven. Do not turn off oven. Cover pork tenderloin with aluminium foil and set aside.
Place peanuts on a baking sheet and roast them in the oven for 5 minutes. Set aside.
Mix all sauce ingredients. Heat in a double boiler and stir continuously.
Cut pork tenderloin into slices. Serve with peanut sauce and roasted peanuts.

Serve with vermicelli noodles or rice.

  * Widely used in Chinese cooking, Hoisin sauce is made with soybeans, garlic, chili peppers and spices.
  ** Japanese rice wine.
 *** A very salty and aromatic liquid condiment, made from salted fermented fish, and used in Asian cuisine as a substitute for salt. In Vietnam it is called nuoc mam, in Thailand nam pla and in Japan shottsuru.
**** Sambal oelek is a sauce made with chili peppers.

All products marked with asterisks are available in supermarkets, Asian grocery stores and fine food shops.

Shrimp and Banana Straddle

Ingredients
1 tsp (5 mL) basil
1 tsp (5 mL) thyme
1 tsp (5 mL) black pepper
1 tsp (5 mL) salt
1 tsp (5 mL) onion powder
1 tsp (5 mL) crushed chili peppers
1 tsp (5 mL) paprika
8 jumbo shrimp
2 tbsp (30 mL) olive oil
8 slices speck*
2 bananas

Method
Mix spices in a small bowl.
Shell the shrimp but leave the last segment of the shell and the tail. Brush with olive oil. Dip in spice mixture and shake to remove excess spices.
Preheat oven on broil.
Peel bananas and cut into 4 chunks. Roll a slice of speck around each chunk.
Skewer bananas and shrimp. Brush with olive oil.
Broil skewers for 5 minutes.

Serve on a bed of basmati rice.

* Speck is a naturally smoked, dry cured ham. It is readily available in delicatessens, but can be replaced with prosciutto (Parma ham).

THE BANANA HAS BEEN DEEMED AN APHRODISIAC, MOSTLY DUE TO ITS SUGGESTIVE SHAPE. IT IS HIGH IN POTASSIUM AND VITAMIN B, WHICH ARE ESSENTIAL TO SEXUAL HORMONE PRODUCTION.

Spicy heat can overwhelm the taste buds. In order to tame the spicy flavours enhanced by an acidic wine, the effects of the spices must be balanced with a wine able to neutralize them. Wines with noticeable sweetness are an irresistible pairing with the spices. It's total submission!

A Bonnezeaux wine from France's Loire Valley region

A white dessert wine from the Jurançon region in South West France

A white wine – a late harvest Riesling from California, USA or the Okanagan Valley in Canada

Ribs For Her Pleasure

Spicy food? Bring on the sturdy wines... extremely sturdy, due to the spices in the marinade. There are a variety of wines at your disposal: Grenache, Tempranillo, Sangiovese, Touriga Nacional, Shiraz and countless others. This orgy of flavours cries out for plenty of smooth and lusty wines to be quaffed with abandon.

A sturdy lager

A "Super Tuscan" red wine from Italy. How can you resist?

A Toro Tempranillo from Spain

Rib Ingredients
1-3/4 lb (800 g) pork ribs
8 cups (2 L) court bouillon*

Marinade Ingredients
2 cups (500 mL) ketchup
1/2 onion, chopped
1 garlic clove, chopped
1/4 cup (65 mL) plum jam
3 tbsp (45 mL) Hoisin sauce**

Method
Simmer pork ribs in the court bouillon over low heat for about 2 hours. Drain and let cool. Place on a baking sheet.
Preheat oven to 375°F (190°C).
Mix marinade ingredients together. Brush pork ribs generously with the marinade.
Bake pork ribs for 30 minutes. Brush ribs with more marinade halfway through cooking.

Serve with homemade french fries.

* Court bouillon is a flavoured liquid for poaching foods. Traditionally, court bouillon is water, bay leaves, carrots, celery, onion, parsley and garlic.

** Widely used in Chinese cooking, Hoisin sauce is made with soybeans, garlic, chili peppers and spices. It is available in supermarkets, Asian food stores and fine food shops.

This recipe of highly contrasting flavours and textures combines Italian, French and North American ingredients. But the wine is decidedly Etruscan. The question is... why Italy? Pure, unadulterated loyalty, of course!

A strong, fragrant Chianti Classico from Tuscany, Italy

A Sangiovese di Romagna from the Emilia-Romagna region in Italy

A Brunello di Montalcino – a highly reputed wine from Tuscany, Italy

Forbidden Pizza

Ingredients

1 pear
2 pats of butter
Sugar, salt and pepper, to taste
1 small Spanish onion
1 tbsp (15 mL) butter
1 tsp (5 mL) sugar
14 oz (400 g) blood sausage, raw
2 thin pizza crusts, 20 cm (8 in) wide
1 cup (250 mL) old or mature cheddar, grated

Method

Preheat oven to 375°F (190°C).
Cut pear in half lengthwise. Core each halved pear and place on a baking sheet.
Add a pat of butter into the hole of each halved pear. Sprinkle with sugar. Season with salt and pepper.
Bake pears for about 10 minutes. Remove from oven and set aside.
Thinly slice Spanish onion. In small pan, caramelize the onion in butter and sugar over medium heat.
Cut blood sausage into thin slices.
Top each pizza crust with half of the caramelized onions and sliced blood sausage. Place a halved pear in the centre of each pizza. Sprinkle grated cheddar evenly over both pizzas.
Bake pizzas for about 10 minutes.

CERTAIN STUDIES SHOW THAT THE AROMA OF CHEESE IS A CONTRIBUTING FACTOR TO ITS REPUTATION AS AN APHRODISIAC. ITS PARTICULAR SCENT PLAYS A ROLE IN SEXUAL AROUSAL. CHEESE IS RICH IN PHENYLETHYLAMINE, WHICH RELEASES A RUSH OF HORMONES SIMILAR TO SEXUAL INTERCOURSE. THEY SAY THE STRONGER THE CHEESE, THE BETTER.

Fondlers Fondue

Ingredients
4-1/2 oz (130 g) Emmental cheese
4-1/2 oz (130 g) Gruyère cheese
4-1/2 oz (130 g) Vacherin Fribourgeois cheese
1 tsp (5 mL) corn starch
1 garlic clove
1 cup (250 mL) amber beer

Method
Grate cheeses. Add corn starch and mix well.
Rub garlic clove all over the inside of a small fondue pot. Leave garlic clove in the pot.
Pour beer into the fondue pot. Heat over medium heat until steam begins to rise.
Reduce heat to low. Add cheese by handfuls, stirring constantly with a wooden spoon in a figure-eight pattern. Serve immediately!

Use day-old baguette bread, cut into cubes, to dip into the fondue. Serve with potatoes, asparagus, ham and dry cured meats.

Arousing, distracting and inviting… your partner's bare legs under the table.

Beer and cheese are a match made in heaven. An unusual pairing? Not at all! They complement each other because they share some of the same flavours. However, the classic pairing is cheese with white wine.

Forget red wine. The fat content in cheese hardens the tannins.

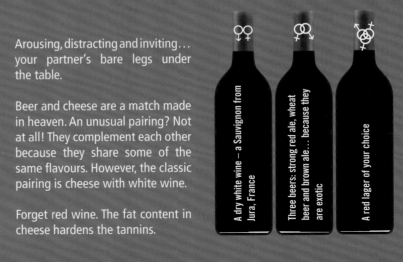

A dry white wine – a Sauvignon from Jura, France

Three beers: strong red ale, wheat beer and brown ale… because they are exotic

A red lager of your choice

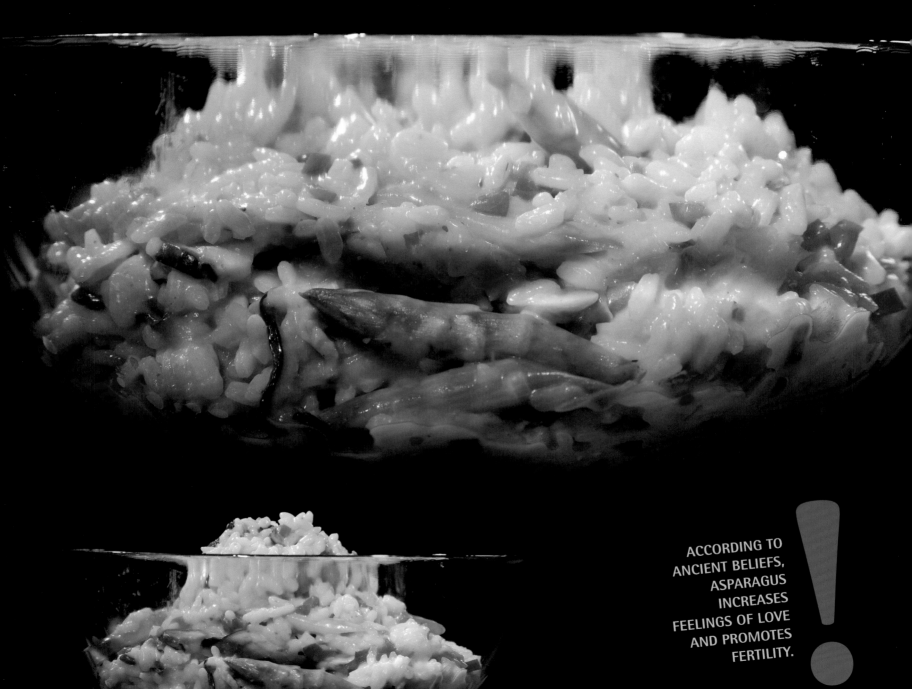

ACCORDING TO
ANCIENT BELIEFS,
ASPARAGUS
INCREASES
FEELINGS OF LOVE
AND PROMOTES
FERTILITY.

Creamy Risotto Eruption

Originally from Italy, risotto has gained in popularity and made its way into kitchens worldwide. Here, the recipe has a tropical twist. This X rated dish of hot and sunny flavours deserves to be washed down elegantly with a sophisticated wine.

A Pinot Grigio white wine from Trentino-Alto Adige, Italy

A white wine from several grape varieties of the Costières de Nîmes appellation, from the Rhône region in France

A white wine – an assemblage of Sauvignon Blanc and Sémillon from Sonoma Valley, USA

Ingredients

6 shiitake mushrooms
1 red pepper, very finely diced the same size
2 grey shallots, finely chopped
Olive oil, as needed
1 cup (250 mL) arborio rice*
1/2 cup (125 mL) dry white wine
3 cups (750 mL) chicken stock
1 cup (250 mL) coconut milk
6 green asparagus, blanched and cut in three
1 tbsp (15 mL) Patak's® Hot Mango Indian Style Pickle**, chopped
Salt and pepper, to taste

Method

Remove stems from mushrooms and thinly slice the caps.
Combine chicken stock and coconut milk in a large saucepan. Bring to a simmer. Keep warm on low heat.
In a large saucepan, sauté red pepper and grey shallot in olive oil over low heat.
Add arborio rice to the vegetables. Deglaze with white wine.
When wine has evaporated, add a ladle of warm broth (or just enough to cover the mixture). Stir continuously with a wooden spoon until all the broth has been absorbed. Repeat process until rice has absorbed all of the broth, about 20 minutes.
Add asparagus a few minutes before cooking time ends, or when there is only one ladle of broth left to stir.
Add hot mango pickles to risotto. Season with salt and pepper. Serve immediately.

* An Italian short-grain rice. Its high starch content gives risotto a creamy consistency.

** Available in the Indian food section of most supermarkets.

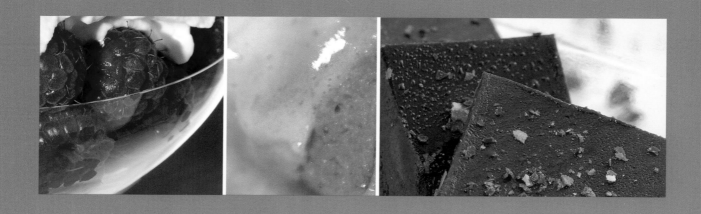

Sweet! Sweet!
Come, come and eat,
For here you'll find
Sweets to your mind.

On every tree
Sugar-plums you'll see;
In every dell
Grows the caramel.

Over every wall
Gum-drops fall;
Molasses flows
Where our river goes.

Under your feet
Lies sugar sweet;
Over your head
Grow almonds red.

And, oh! what bliss
When two friends kiss,
For they honey sip
From lip to lip!

Extract from Sweet! Sweet!
Louisa May Alcott (1832-1888)

Guilty Pleasures

A deep, rich, satisfying coffee served to your beloved with tenderness and elegance. Sweet fortified wines and dessert wines are also tantalizing accompaniments of the finest order.

Coffee... a rich double espresso with woody or chocolaty flavours

A sherry made from Pedro Ximénez (PX) grapes, Spain

An LBV Port from Douro, Portugal

Naughty Coffee Indulgence

Ingredients
1 bag mini marshmallows [9 oz (250 g)]
1 cup (250 mL) hot water, in total
4 tsp (20 mL) instant coffee
2 cups (500 mL) 35% cream or whipping cream
1/4 cup (65 mL) sugar
1 tsp (5 mL) vanilla extract
1 package thin chocolate cookies [7 oz (200 g)]
1/4 cup (65 mL) unsalted butter, softened
Dark chocolate 54% cocoa or milk chocolate shavings

Method
In a medium saucepan, heat 3/4 cup (190 mL) water over low heat. Add marshmallows. Stir marshmallows with a wooden spoon until they melt. Transfer to a medium-sized bowl. In a small bowl, dissolve instant coffee in 1/4 cup (65 mL) hot water. Add coffee to melted marshmallows.
Refrigerate mixture for one hour, stirring occasionally (2 or 3 times) to keep texture smooth. Whisk cream, sugar and vanilla extract to make whipped cream. Set aside.
In a 9-inch (23 cm) springform pan, place cookies vertically against the sides of the pan. Make crumbs with remaining cookies by placing them in a resealable plastic bag and crushing them with a rolling pin.
In a medium-sized bowl, work the butter into the crumbs with a fork until the butter is evenly distributed.
Press crust evenly onto the bottom of the springform pan.
Remove marshmallow mixture from the refrigerator. Whisk for about 30 seconds until smooth again.
Gently fold whipped cream into this mixture.
Pour mixture into springform pan and top with chocolate shavings.
Refrigerate for 12 hours.

Hot and ready
At the tip of your stick
Yes, eat me up like candy
                    Erotica

Warm Marshmallow Caress

Ingredients

6 gelatine leaves* (10 g)
1/2 cup (125 mL) water
1 cup (250 mL) sugar
1/3 cup (85 mL) blackberry juice
1 egg white

Method

Line a baking sheet with oiled parchment paper.

To make syrup, combine water and sugar in a deep saucepan. Bring mixture to a boil, stirring often, until temperature on a candy thermometer reaches 260°F (125°C). Ensure mixture does not overflow.

In a small bowl, soak gelatine leaves in cold water until softened. Squeeze out excess water.

Meanwhile, in another saucepan, heat blackberry juice over low heat. Add gelatine leaves.

Using a mixer, beat egg white until soft peaks form.

When syrup is ready, gradually add a thin stream of hot blackberry juice while stirring continuously. Then slowly pour mixture on the egg white while beating constantly. Continue beating mixture for another 5 minutes.

Pour mixture evenly on baking sheet. Cover with oiled parchment paper and plastic wrap and refrigerate overnight (about 12 hours).

Gently remove the parchment paper from the marshmallow and cut into different-sized pieces.

Place marshmallow pieces on a stick. Toast with a kitchen torch or place under the broiler. Serve.

* Gelatine leaves are available in most supermarkets and fine food shops. Each .35 oz (10 g) package contains 6 sheets.

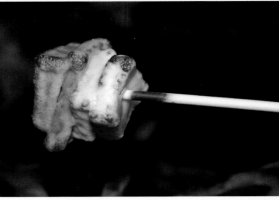

Just one: a hydromel – a mead / honey wine flavoured with maple and blueberries

The wine selected must match its accompaniment. In tasting, the mouth must remain faithful to the nose. The result should be a pleasant wine with a long and unctuous finish. Surprise! It's a hydromel! A most delicious discovery!

CHOCOLATE
RELEASES
PLEASURE
HORMONES.
CASANOVA DRANK
SEVERAL CUPS
OF CHOCOLATE
BEFORE BEDDING
HIS CONQUESTS.

Chocolate and Banana Ecstacy

Chocolate Ecstacy Ingredients

Softened butter, as needed
Cocoa powder, as needed
2 oz (57 g) dark chocolate 70% cocoa
2 tbsp (30 mL) unsalted butter
4 tbsp (60 mL) sugar
2 eggs
3 tbsp (45 mL) all-purpose flour

Method

Grease two 3-inch (7.5 cm) ramekins with the softened butter.
Dust with cocoa powder.
Preheat oven to 400°F (205°C).
Melt chocolate and unsalted butter in a double boiler. Set aside.
Beat the egg yolks and sugar until creamy and pale in colour.
Fold chocolate mixture into egg mixture. Sift in flour while whisking.
Pour mixture into the ramekins. Bake for 12 to 14 minutes.
Remove from ramekins and serve with a banana milkshake.

Banana Milkshake Ingredients

1 banana
1/2 cup (125 mL) milk
1/2 cup (125 mL) vanilla ice cream

Method

Blend all ingredients in a blender. Serve immediately.

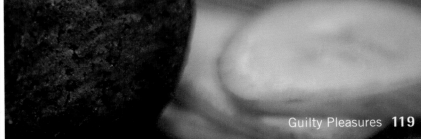

Ladyfinger Strokes

Ingredients

2 tbsp (30 mL) sugar
1 egg yolk
1 egg white
2 tbsp (30 mL) mascarpone cheese
1/2 cup (125 mL) 35% cream or whipping cream
1 tbsp (15 mL) Tia Maria®
4 ladyfingers
1 cup of coffee, at room temperature
1 container [6 oz (170 g)] raspberries
Cocoa powder, to taste

Method

Beat the egg white until soft peaks form. Set aside.
Whip the cream and set aside.
In a bowl, beat the egg yolk and sugar until creamy and
pale in colour.
Add mascarpone cheese and Tia Maria. Mix well.
Gently fold egg white, then whipped cream, into this mixture.
To serve, use two large glasses with a
7/8 cup (220 mL) capacity.
Fill each glass with alternate layers: ladyfingers
dipped in coffee and cut in half, raspberries,
and creamy mixture. Then dust lightly with
cocoa powder.

This is the Italian "dessert of love" so bring
on the seductive wine. Words are no longer
necessary. Action!

A Passito di Pantelleria from Sicily, Italy

A Sauternes dessert wine from Bordeaux, France

A sweet fortified wine – a Muscat de Rivesaltes from the Roussillon region in France

VANILLA'S AROMA IS WHAT GIVES IT ITS APHRODISIAC QUALITIES. THIS IS WHY IT IS OFTEN USED TO MAKE PERFUME. IN COUNTRIES LIKE VENEZUELA, MEXICO AND ARGENTINA, A FEW VANILLA BEANS ARE SOAKED IN A GLASS OF TEQUILA FOR ALMOST A MONTH. THE RESULT? VIM AND VIGOUR!

Up All Night Delight

Ingredients

1-1/2 leaves (2 g) gelatine*
1 vanilla bean
1-1/4 cups (315 mL) 35% cream or whipping cream
2 tbsp (30 mL) sugar
1 tbsp (15 mL) sugar syrup**
1 passion fruit
4 mint leaves
1 tbsp (15 mL) grapeseed oil

Method

Soak gelatine leaves in cold water for about 5 minutes.
Cut the vanilla bean lengthwise. Scrape the seeds free from both sides of the bean with the edge of the knife.
Heat cream, sugar and vanilla in a small saucepan over low heat.
Squeeze out excess water from gelatine leaves. Add to heated cream mixture while whisking.
Pour mixture into small ramekins and refrigerate for 2 hours.
Cut passion fruit in half. Scoop out pulp and set aside.
Chop mint leaves and mix with grapeseed oil.
Top cooled cream mixture with sugar syrup, passion fruit pulp and minted oil.

*   Gelatine leaves are available in most supermarkets and fine food shops. Each .35 oz (10 g) package contains 6 sheets.

** Sugar syrup: Boil 3/8 cup (95 mL) water and 1/2 cup (125 mL) sugar for 2 minutes. Allow to cool. This sugared water can be refrigerated for several weeks and is ideal for sweetening cocktails!

A food and wine pairing inextricably linked to Italy, deemed the country of love. One can't argue with this intoxicating bond, whether it's truth or fallacy.

A definite must! An Italian dessert wine... sweet, inviting, exotic, exciting, even arousing. Good for sharing, but also enjoyable alone.

A sweet fortified wine – a Passito di Pantelleria from Sicily, Italy

A Vespaiola from Veneto, Italy

A Vin Santo di Montepulciano from Tuscany, Italy

Have you beheld (with much delight)
A red rose peeping through a white?
Or else a cherry (double graced)
Within a lily? Centre placed?
Or ever marked the pretty beam,
A strawberry shows, half drowned in cream?
Or seen rich rubies blushing through
A pure smooth pearl, and orient too?
So like to this, nay all the rest,
Is each neat niplet of her breast.

Robert Herrick (1591-1674)

Peach Bosom Tarts

Ingredients

1/3 cup (85 mL) sugar
1 tbsp (15 mL) water
2 canned peach halves
1/4 cup (65 mL) chopped walnuts
1 pinch ground ginger
1 pinch ground nutmeg
Puff pastry, as needed

Method

Preheat oven to 350°F (175°C).
In a small saucepan, mix sugar and water. Heat over medium heat, without stirring, until a reddish-brown caramel forms.
Pour the caramel into two small tart molds of 3 inches (7 cm) in diameter.
Fill each mold with a peach half, pitted side up.
Place walnuts, ginger and nutmeg into the hole of each halved peach.
Cover peach halves with puff pastry. Bake for 15 minutes or until pastry is golden brown.
Remove molds from the oven and turn over immediately into serving dishes.
Serve with vanilla ice cream.

This dessert is truly deserving of a sweet fortified wine that will bring out the aroma of peach also present in the wine. Peach aromas, as well as apricot, are indications of high quality wine. Pamper your taste buds and experience pure bliss!

A Vouvray aged dessert wine or a Coteaux du Layon, from France's Loire Valley region

A Canadian ice wine. They are all delicious

A Côtes de Provence or Tavel rosé from France

Marriage of Truffles

Ingredients

7 oz (200 g) dark chocolate 70% cocoa
1.75 oz (50 g) icing sugar
3/8 cup (95 mL) 35% cream or whipping cream
1 egg yolk
1/2 tsp (2.5 mL) Espelette pepper
3.5 oz (100 g) butter, cut into cubes
1 tbsp (15 mL) cocoa powder
A pinch of Espelette pepper

Method

Melt chocolate in a double boiler.
Add sugar, cream, egg yolk and Espelette pepper.
Whisk and remove from heat.
Still whisking, add cubes of butter, one at a time.
Pour mixture into a 5-inch (12 cm) square pan, very tightly covered with plastic wrap.
Cool in the refrigerator for 2 hours.
Mix cocoa powder and pinch of Espelette pepper.
Dip a knife in hot water.
Cut into squares and sprinkle with cocoa-pepper blend.

Champagne and chocolate are mostly associated with celebration rather than a successful food and wine match. In fact, chocolate and champagne don't pair all that well.

Nevertheless, there are exceptions. For example, a champagne without citrus and mineral freshness, with a high percentage of red grapes (75% Pinot Noir or Pinot Meunier), that is to say, a lightly oxidized champagne with tobacco and cinnamon notes. If there is a bitter mouthfeel, then dark chocolate makes a good partner.

Taste it just for the pleasure. And if you don't like it, drink the rest of the bottle from your partner's belly button.

A sweet fortified red wine – a Maury from the Roussillon region in France

A Beaumes de Venise Muscat from France's southern Rhône region

A brut champagne as previously described

Laughing, *drinking*
Straight from the bottle
You penetrate me
With intensity
Flowing from your lips
I feel in my throat
This quintessential nectar

Den Hall
(Translated from the French)

Fruity Vibrations

Ingredients

8 gelatine leaves* (13.5 g)
1/2 vanilla bean
1 star anise
1 cinnamon stick
1/4 cup (65 mL) sugar
1 cup (250 mL) water
2 cups (500 mL) juice of preference (apple, grape, cranberry or strawberry)

Method

In a small bowl, soak gelatine leaves in cold water for about 5 minutes.
In a medium saucepan, bring vanilla, star anise, cinnamon, sugar and water to a boil.
Simmer syrup for 5 minutes. Remove from heat.
Squeeze out excess water from gelatine leaves. Add to half of the flavoured syrup**.
Add fruit juice to syrup.
Pour into molds and refrigerate for 2 hours***.

* Gelatine leaves are available in most supermarkets and fine food shops. Each .35 oz (10 g) package contains 6 sheets.

** The other half of the flavoured syrup can be used to repeat the recipe with another type of juice.

*** Dip molds in hot water to make unmolding easier. This needs to be done quickly or the gelatine will melt.

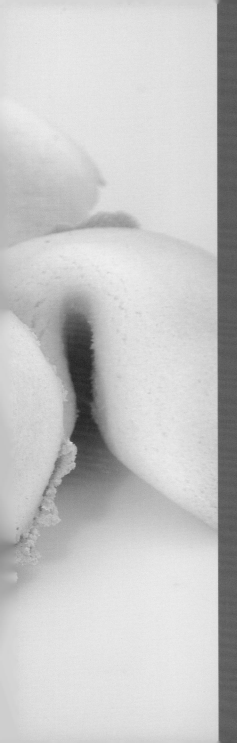

Suggestive Little Bundles

Ingredients

3 tbsp (45 mL) all-purpose flour
2 egg whites
1/3 cup (85 mL) sugar
3 tbsp (45 mL) corn starch
1/2 tsp (2.5 mL) vanilla extract
1 tsp (5 mL) walnut oil

Method

Preheat oven to 350°F (175°C).
Write suggestive messages on little strips of paper, approximately 1-1/2 inches x 1/2 inch (4 cm x 1 cm).
In a medium sized-bowl, beat egg whites until foamy.
Add sugar, corn starch and flour, then vanilla extract and walnut oil.
On a well greased baking sheet or one that has been covered with a baking mat, drop 2 tsp (10 mL) batter for each 3 or 4-inch circle (8 to 10 cm).
Bake for 4 to 5 minutes.
Remove cookies with a spatula.
Place a message in the centre of each cookie. Fold edge of cookie over to make a semi circle.
To give cookie its curved shape, fold each cookie over the edge of the baking sheet.
Let cookies cool at room temperature.

Tea for two? It's the ideal match for these deliciously intriguing message holders.

A black tea from India – a Darjeeling, for example

A Japanese green tea, such as a Sencha Isagawa

A lightly oxidized tea, like an Oolong from China

With my tongue, I touch you
I suck and savour, I do
You melt in my mouth
Slowly, no way out

Erotica

Icy Tongue Teasers

Yogurt Version Ingredients

1 cup (250 mL) strawberries, frozen
1 cup (250 mL) vanilla yogurt
1/2 cup (125 mL) peach juice
4 tbsp (60 mL) honey
Juice of 1/2 lime
Ground long pepper, to taste

Method

Puree all ingredients in a blender until smooth.
Pour mixture into six popsicle molds with a 3/8 cup (95 mL) capacity each. Freeze for at least 2 hours.
To make unmolding easier, run molds under hot water for a few seconds.

Fruit Version Ingredients

Oranges, as many needed to make 1 cup (250 mL) juice
1-1/2 cups (375 mL) mango pulp, frozen
4 tbsp (60 mL) maple syrup

Method

Scrape the zest from the oranges. Blanch zests by bringing water in a small saucepan to a boil. Add zests and remove with a perforated spoon. Rinse immediately under cold water. Repeat process four times. (It removes the bitter taste). Set aside.
Squeeze oranges.
Puree orange juice, mango pulp and maple syrup in a blender until smooth. Add blanched zests to the mixture.
Pour mixture into six popsicle molds with a 3/8 cup (95 mL) capacity each. Freeze for at least 2 hours.
To make unmolding easier, run molds under hot water for a few seconds.

Variation

Substitute frozen fruit with fresh seasonal fruit, locally sourced if possible.
For an original twist, make layered popsicles with different types of juice by freezing one layer at a time.
Wooden sticks can be used instead of the plastic handles in the popsicle molds. Insert sticks half way though the freezing process (after about 1 hour).

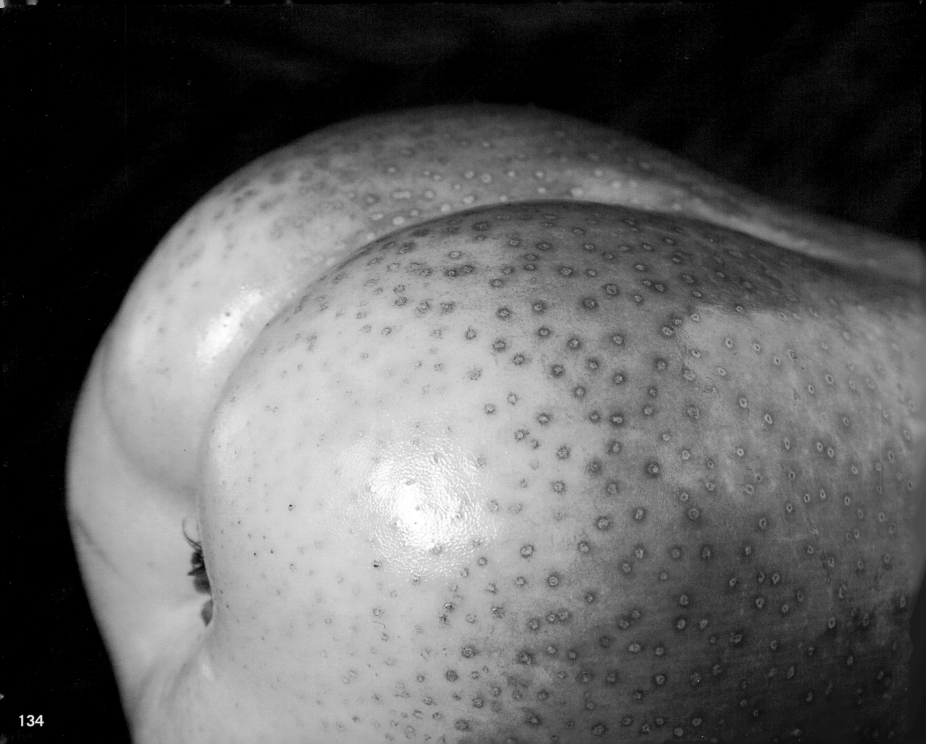

Index

A Thousand Thanks!

• **Stark & Whyte** (www.starketwhyte.com), for the fabulous kitchen accessories. • **Marie-France and Tania, of 12° en Cave** (www.12encave.com), for the glassware and wine accessories. • **Daniel, of Camellia Sinensis tea store** (www.camellia-sinensis.com), for confirming the food and tea pairings. • **Blush Lingerie** (www.blushlingerie.com), for the lingerie. • **Le Château** (www.lechateau.ca), for the clothes. • **Bijouterie Moug**, for the jewellery. • **Roche Bobois** (www.rochebobois.com), for the furniture. • **Shark Agency** (www.shark-agency.com), for the models. • **The members of IDI2 production company (Marc, Anne-Marie, Félipe , Sophie, Julie, Mathilde and Fabien)**, for their professionalism. **The models: Cynthia, Mylène, Léa, Anne-Marie, Vanessa, Carl, Salomée, Christian, Stéphanie and Samuel** • **Conrad Morin**, for his love of wine and his critical eye. • **Véronique Dalle**, for introducing me to the two chefs, and for showing such kindness. • **Phil**, for his love and inspiration. • **Manon, Hélène, Dominique, Renée, Luce, Richard, Michel, Luc and Mr. Perrotte**, for their loyal friendship. • **My elderly parents**, for their love. • **Renée, Victor and Pierre**, for their music selections. • **Danielle**, for being such a good listener and for her love and devotion to Alain. • **Pierre**, for a man's opinion on Sonia's artistic work.